Endorsements for
Highways of Holiness

Intriguing, informing, engrossing, inspiring, provocative, promise-filled, motivational—those are just a few words to describe my dear friend Lloyd Turner's breakthrough book. He raises Christ's glory high, and invites us to walk His high-way of revival with brand new eyes. Since much of his historical material is taken from my backyard, I can assure you that I will never look at metro New York the same again. Lloyd's template will help you, too, to better pursue Christ for a spiritual awakening in the communities where you live.

David Bryant
Author, *CHRIST IS ALL! A Joyful Manifesto on the Supremacy of God's Son* (ChristIsAllBook.com)

I am convinced that God is doing a special thing as we see Highways of Holiness being raised across the globe. Across Africa, from Cape to Cairo, and in many places around the world, I am excited about this great challenge, which is put to us in Isaiah 62:10. Lloyd has taken this challenge, and I pray that God will raise a Highway of Holiness over the Northeast as the marketplace leaders "humble themselves and pray . . ." (2 Chronicles 7:14). May we see a *great* revival emanate from this region in the foreseeable future.

Graham Power
Global Day of Prayer Chairperson
CEO, Power Group of Companies
Cape Town, South Africa

Get on board and enjoy a ride on Route 78 in New Jersey, where the Spirit of God has dug some remarkable wells of revival. *Highways of Holiness* is truly a complete work that marks a new beginning for prayer warriors seeking to pray effectual prayers that will lead to a fresh move of God. If you believe that what you learn from the past can influence your prayer life toward a future hope, you will be blessed to take in all that Lloyd Turner has put before you in this outstanding textbook. Filled with resources and ideas, this book serves as a model that will result in Highways of Holiness all over our nation.
So sit back, get comfortable, and let God arise!

Patricia L. Wenzel
Founder and Director, PRAY New Jersey, Inc.
New Jersey State Coordinator, National Day of Prayer
Oak Ridge, New Jersey

When I heard Lloyd Turner talk about "Highways of Holiness," my eyes were wide open, my heart was pounding, and I wanted to hear all he had to say. Everyone in the room was leaning into his words. Why? Because he was showing us the history of God moving in New Jersey and how God wants to move again. *Highways of Holiness* develops principles from past spiritual awakenings and applies them to the present in an easy-to-understand framework. If you want to see your city reached for Christ, this is a must-read.

Jack Serra
Author, *Marketplace, Marriage and Revival:*
The Spiritual Connection
Vice President of Ministry, Harvest Evangelism, Inc.
Founder and President, "The M&M Connection"

In *Highways of Holiness* Lloyd Turner documents the moves of God that have occurred along Interstate 78, which traverses New York and New Jersey. He calls Route 78 a Highway of Holiness, and encourages us to look for Highways of Holiness in our own lives. Lloyd has also observed the effectiveness of the biblical principles of Prayer Evangelism (Luke 10:1–9, 17–18) in operation in Argentina. In the context of his historical analysis, he sees enormous potential for the application of these principles along Interstate 78. I look forward to helping him redig these wells of revival.

Rick Heeren
Regional Vice President, Harvest Evangelism, Inc.
Minnesota Coordinator, United States Strategic Prayer Network
Editor and Compiler, *The Elk River Story*
Author, *Thank God It's Monday!*

Awesome! *Highways of Holiness* is an extraordinary book with a lot of insight in the way of Holiness. This book prepares the saints to open Revival Wells that have been clogged for centuries. Please read this book with a receptive heart and be part of the coming Revival.

Rev. Conway & Joan Simmons
Richard Allen AME Church
St. George's, Bermuda

Be forewarned: What you are about to read will convict, inspire, and convince you to rededicate yourself to do whatever it takes to birth revival. Anything less may mean the demise of our nation.

Fran Huber
Pastor, First Christian Assembly and
New Jersey Faith Alliance

In *Highways of Holiness* Lloyd Turner brings a clarion call to the church of New Jersey and, as such, to the church of America. It takes us from the facts of our past, moves us to grasp their context, and from there quickly ushers us into strategy development. There is an "Aha" moment coming for an awakened church in this state, and Lloyd's book brings us one giant step closer to seeing that come into reality. *Highways of Holiness* provides much-needed insights for those looking for the Lord's coming.

Pat Busch
Team Leader of Missions Outreach
The Philadelphia Church
Oak Ridge, New Jersey

Highways of Holiness is absolutely remarkable! Lloyd Turner passionately mines some of the deep, rich spiritual history of his New Jersey stomping grounds and brilliantly connects it to a more remarkable future surely soon to come. In these pages he reveals timeless and transferable principles that give us faith to build our own Highways of Holiness for our cities.

David E. Thompson
Sr. Vice President, Harvest Evangelism, Inc.

Highways of Holiness

HIGHWAYS
of
HOLINESS

Preparing the Way for the Lord

LLOYD TURNER

**A Transformational Publications Book
Division of Harvest Evangelism, Inc.**

**"And a highway will be there;
it will be called the Way of Holiness."
—Isaiah 35:8**

Copyright ©2006, 2013 by Lloyd Turner
All rights reserved
Self-published with CreateSpace by Lloyd Turner
A publication of Transformational Publications
A Division of Harvest Evangelism, Inc.
PO Box 20310, San Jose CA 95160-0310
Tel. 408-927-9052
www.harvestevan.org
**ISBN-13: 978-1492993698
ISBN-10: 1492993697**

Contents

Introduction: Reaffirming an Ancient Covenant /9

When we come into agreement with the godly covenants made by our ancestors, we reaffirm God's divine purposes and blessings for our family, city, and nation. This reaffirmation of past covenants allows us to achieve a "synergy of the ages." In so doing we acknowledge that God continues to honor sacred covenants made in earlier generations.

PART ONE: Preparing the Way

1   Redigging the Ancient Wells /17

Stones of remembrance are historical markers that remind us of past events. These markers also provide clues about God's purposes for a city or region. By studying these stones of remembrance, we can discover ancient wells of revival that may have been stopped up. When these wells are unclogged, God promises to open up fresh springs of living water.

2   The Spirit of the Lord and Revival /27

Isaiah 11:2 describes seven aspects of the Holy Spirit that were poured out on Jesus—the Spirit of the LORD, wisdom, understanding, counsel, power, knowledge, and fear of the LORD. These same aspects of the Spirit are released during times of revival. To understand how these

1

aspects of the Spirit operate today, we need to step out of our human-centered worldview and consider spiritual awakenings from God's perspective. The Prayer Evangelism model shows how we can use biblical principles to transform the spiritual climate in cities and nations.

4/ *Highways of Holiness*

9 The Clouds Will be Rolled Back /153

The First Great Awakening ended abruptly in 1743 when "threatening clouds" of opposition rolled into New England. Edwards and others believed that harsh judgments by some revivalists had quenched this move of God. He believed that a wind from the west would roll away these dark clouds from New England one day. After that the Sun of Righteousness will come in from the east, ushering in the last, greatest, worldwide revival.

10 Restoring All That Was Lost /165

The lower Hudson Valley was indescribably beautiful when Henry Hudson and his crew landed in 1609. The Indians initially welcomed the Dutch settlers in New Amsterdam, but relationships quickly deteriorated after a series of massacres. The Highways of Holiness strategy is proposed to restore all that was lost—man's relationships to the land, to the marketplace, to other people, and to the Creator.

    A. Scriptures About the Highway of Holiness
    B. "Divident Hill" by Mrs. E. C. Kinney
    C. Jonathan Edwards' Observations on Revival
    D. Wells of Revival on Interstate 78

Scripture Index /205

General Index /207

Foreword

In the years since our first city-reaching efforts began in Resistencia, Argentina, in 1988, Harvest Evangelism has had the privilege of developing and equipping leaders for marketplace, city, and nation transformation through transferable strategies and prototypes. We developed these key themes in our books *That None Should Perish, Prayer Evangelism,* and *Anointed for Business* (Regal Books). Thousands of men and women have learned how to reach cities, nations, and businesses for Jesus Christ through our books, seminars, and international conferences.

Through Transformational Publications, Harvest Evangelism seeks to elaborate on these principles through the insights and experiences of practitioners. My friend Lloyd Turner is one of those practitioners, and his book, *Highways of Holiness,* builds on that foundation. In this book, Lloyd extends the model of Prayer Evangelism that Jesus provides in Luke chapter 10, showing that believers are called to walk along a highway that is both physical and spiritual. He challenges us to apply the instructions found in Isaiah 62:10–12 to restore individuals, cities, and nations to their intended reflection of the glory of God, wherever we live.

In Section One he shows how the Lord led him to discover fourteen historic "wells of revival" located along Interstate 78 in New Jersey. As he prayed for the Lord to redig these wells, he realized he was being called to adopt Interstate 78 as his own Highway of Holiness.

The second section of the book provides four case studies describing how God has moved during past spiritual awakenings along this particular highway. Lloyd documents how, as Christians prayed for the needs of their cities in these prior revivals, the Holy Spirit provided new and remarkable ways of drawing men and women to Jesus Christ. Moreover, as we examine the still unanswered prayer requests of former generations, we are encouraged to come into agreement with the godly covenants that were made during those spiritual awakenings.

The third section of the book offers a model for building up our own Highway of Holiness. Lloyd describes seven steps that are involved in constructing a spiritual highway, then shows how Highways of Holiness help the Body of Christ to prepare for the last, greatest revival that will come on earth. In that revival the Lord will remove the present clouds of darkness and will restore all the relationships that were lost in the Fall of Man.

The pattern and teaching of the Scriptures is clear: Jesus came to seek and to save all that which was lost (Luke 19:10, NASB). Our assignment from the Lord is to reclaim what He has already redeemed by taking the power and the presence of the Lord to the highways and byways of our cities and nations. The principles revealed in this book will lead you confidently to build your own "Highway of Holiness." Be blessed as you read on!

Ed Silvoso
President, Harvest Evangelism
Author

Acknowledgments

I would like to thank several individuals and organizations for their contributions to this book. First, I thank those who have prayed faithfully for the Kingdom of God to advance in the state of New Jersey. Particular thanks go to Aglow International, Lydia Fellowship International, the New Jersey Faith Alliance, PRAY New Jersey, New Jersey Strategic Prayer Command, and the New Jersey Global Apostolic Prayer Network (formerly the New Jersey Strategic Prayer Network). These and other prayer organizations are to be commended for their faithful prayers and watch over New Jersey for many years.

Special thanks are due to Ed Silvoso and his colleagues at Harvest Evangelism. Ed's books entitled **Prayer Evangelism** and **Anointed for Business** have produced key prototypes that are used in this book. Dave Thompson, who heads the Transformational Publications Division of Harvest Evangelism, deserves particular thanks for the countless email messages and phone conversations related to this book, and for his administrative leadership and prayers in seeing this project to completion. Thanks, too, to Jack Serra for his encouragement in launching this project and his numerous suggestions at key points.

To David Bryant, for his thoughtful review of my manuscript, and for suggestions about how to improve its focus and content.

To Jane Rumph, who edited the manuscript thoughtfully and with the highest professional standards.

7

To Steve Martin, who provided the cover designs and sketches for this book.

To my wife, Joanne, who is my best friend and a loving critic. She has been telling me for years that I needed to write a book like this!

And finally, to my faithful "cloud of witnesses" who have been praying that this book would be completed in a way that exalts Jesus Christ. You know who you are!

Reaffirming an Ancient Covenant

Coming into Agreement Across the Generations

Newark and Elizabeth are two of the oldest cities in New Jersey. Both were founded by Puritan immigrants from Connecticut who settled in New Jersey in the year 1666. These communities grew very quickly, and during the next two years questions began to arise about the legal boundaries between them. Consequently, on May 20, 1668, nine of the founders of Newark and Elizabeth (or Elizabethtown, as it was originally called) agreed on the dividing lines between these cities and made a solemn declaration to honor these boundaries in perpetuity.

These men were founders of their respective cities who represented government, religious, and commercial sectors. Their stature and achievements were impressive:

- Robert Treat and Jasper Crane were Newark's first two *magistrates* (mayors). Treat was both the *temporal and spiritual leader* of Newark until First Church called a permanent pastor. He returned to Connecticut in 1672 and served as governor of that state for thirty-two years. Crane worked with Treat to lay out the first city plot for Newark

9

and became magistrate after Treat's move back to Connecticut. He was also a landowner and **merchant** in Newark.

- Matthias Camfield became the first **auditor** of Newark's treasury in 1668.

- Richard Harrison was a wealthy landowner who **constructed and operated Newark's first grist mill.**

- Thomas Johnson was the first appointed **constable** of Newark. He owned the city's first inn and held exclusive rights to the **sale of liquor** in the city.

- John Ogden was a prominent **founder** of Elizabethtown who became that city's **representative to the first New Jersey Assembly.**

- Luke Watson was one of the **real estate entrepreneurs** who purchased 500,000 acres of land from the Indians. This land included not only Elizabethtown but also all of Union County and parts of Somerset and Morris Counties.

- Robert Bond and Jeffrey Jones were two prominent landowners who formed the Elizabethtown Associates **real estate business** in 1664.

At the signing of the agreement, John Ogden recalled that Governor Treat made a declaration that day "that if the Newark people differed with the Elizabethtown people concerning that line, that he believed they would never prosper."[1] Unfortunately, however, a prior claim to a small triangle of land near Divident Hill was discovered a few years later, and the leaders from Newark demanded that this land be transferred to their city. This triangle of land was transferred several times until it was permanently annexed by Newark in 1902—nearly 250 years after the 1668 prayer meeting.

Today, both of these cities are struggling with problems of crime, unemployment, and the need for economic renewal. When several intercessors from New Jersey began to sense that Newark was the key to restoring prosperity in the Garden State, the idea of rededicating these former Puritan cities was suggested. Accordingly, on the morning of June 10, 2004, twenty-four pastors and intercessors (including the author) met at Divident Hill to renew the covenant made at this historic site in 1668. We read the poem "Divident Hill,"[2] which was written during the 19th century, and many of us began to sense that a spiritual battle was occurring in our midst. As we continued to lift up praise, worship, and prayers for Newark and Elizabeth, a sense of peace and joy came upon us. One intercessor said she saw "angels ascending and descending" through the cupola at the top of the monument, and another saw "an image of God's face, smiling down upon us" as we interceded for these two colonial-era cities.

Those who attended the 2004 rededication at Divident Hill experienced the power of coming into agreement with God's eternal purposes for Newark and Elizabeth. While we read these ancient covenants, and realized that God still honored them, we experienced a beautiful illustration of the concept of the "synergy of the ages." We understood that the covenants had been broken by man, not by God, and that God still wants to bring peace and prosperity to these two early cities. The "synergy of the ages," according to authors Dutch Sheets and Will Ford, occurs when believers proclaim and honor covenants that God made with previous generations.[3] Although we did not understand everything that happened in the heavenlies that day, we realized that God's hand was heavy over that historic monument as we repeated prayers and poems that spanned 350 years of New Jersey's history. Divident Hill is still a "high place" that can be used to usher the Kingdom of God into Newark and Elizabeth.

"DIVIDENT HILL" – DIVIDING NEWARK AND ELIZABETHTOWN

In 1668 the founders of Newark and Elizabeth(town) declared a covenant of peace during a prayer meeting at Divident Hill.[4]

Preparing the Way for the Lord

The pages that follow will show us how to prepare for the next great movement of God in revival. The book is divided into three parts. Part One, called "Preparing the Way," describes how we can prepare our hearts and minds for the next great move of God. Chapter One continues the topic of agreement across the ages by examining several wells of revival in New Jersey. In Chapter Two we suggest that there are three distinct types of revival, and the key factor that determines the course of the revival is which aspects (or operations) of the Holy Spirit are dominant at that point in time. Chapter Three introduces the concept of a "Highway of Holiness" and why it is important in preparing for the next move of God. In this chapter particular emphasis is given to my own personal Highway of Holiness.

Part Two is called "Past Awakenings." It includes Chapters Four through Seven, which describe four stops along my Highway of

Holiness (Martins Creek, Pennsylvania; Basking Ridge, New Jersey; New Providence, New Jersey; and New York City) where God has produced spiritual awakenings in past generations.

Part Three, entitled "Your Highway of Holiness," describes how you can become an agent of transformation in your personal sphere of influence. Chapter Eight discusses how you can apply these ideas to prepare the way for your own Highway of Holiness. Chapter Nine describes how we can come into agreement with 18th century prayers for a spiritual awakening that will turn back the clouds of darkness in the United States and other nations. And finally Chapter Ten concludes this book by reviewing how the land becomes defiled and what intercessors, pastors, and marketplace ministers can do "to seek and to save that which was lost" (Luke 19:10, NASB).

May the Lord bless you on your journey as richly as He has blessed my travels along the Highway of Holiness!

PRAYER

Father, we are thankful that you are a covenant-keeping God. Although our knowledge of your past covenants with our forefathers is limited, we believe that you remember and honor all your promises to past generations. Make us aware of the covenants you have made with men and women in our region, so that we might come into agreement with these holy proclamations. And as we reaffirm your sacred covenants, we pray that you would rend the heavens and come down to earth in this generation. We approach you as little children coming to Jesus, in whose name we pray. Amen.

PART ONE

PREPARING THE WAY

CHAPTER ONE

Redigging the Ancient Wells

Isaac reopened the wells that had been dug in the time of his father Abraham, which the Philistines had stopped up after Abraham died, and he gave them the same names his father had given them.
—Genesis 26:18

What Happened Here?

In 1983 I left the field of higher education to become a management consultant at AT&T. After six years of teaching public policy analysis, I felt the Lord leading me to become a consultant to large corporations. It was a timely move and one I have never regretted.

Shortly after my move from Pennsylvania to New Jersey, my parents came out from the Midwest to visit me for a week. Dad and Mom were both historians, having met each other in graduate school at the University of Iowa. So they were full of questions when I drove them around the quaint colonial towns that are scattered throughout New Jersey.

"There's a historical marker about the Old Dutch Parsonage," Dad exclaimed as I drove him through Somerville. "What happened here?" he asked me.

"Beats me," I replied. "I just moved into the area and haven't had a chance to do much sightseeing. I'll let you know if I learn more about that place."

That day I began to realize that New Jersey is saturated with signs, markers, and stones to commemorate its rich colonial legacy. Many of these, including the Old Dutch Parsonage, remind us that the affairs of church and state have been closely interlinked throughout the history of the United States. This particular parsonage, as I later learned, was adjacent to George Washington's residence and military center during the winter of 1778–79. His Continental Army was outnumbered by the British Army that occupied the American Colonies, and so he retreated to the Watchung Mountains of New Jersey to spend the long winter while planning his strategies for the next year.

During that winter Washington stayed in a private home next to the parsonage occupied by Dominie (Pastor) Jacob Hardenbergh, who led a small but thriving congregation at the Dutch Reformed Church in nearby Raritan. Hardenbergh's congregation strongly supported the Continental Army cause and provided land for the troops to camp along the Raritan River. Washington and Hardenbergh became cordial friends that winter, and at the end of his stay, Washington wrote a thank-you to the Raritan congregation, stating,

> *I thank you, gentlemen, sincerely for the sense you entertain of the conduct of the army, and for the interest you take in my welfare. I trust the goodness of the cause, and the exertions of the people, under Divine protection, will give us that honorable peace for which we are contending. Suffer me, gentlemen, to wish the Reformed Church at Raritan a long continuance of its present minister and consistory, and all the blessings which flow from piety and religion.* [1]   —G. Washington, June 2, 1779

A few miles from the Old Dutch Parsonage is the gravestone of the Reverend Theodorus Frelinghuysen, who was the first Dutch Reformed minister in the Raritan Valley. In 1720 four congregations called him from Holland to lead their churches, and he began to preach to them about spiritual renewal and the need to be "born again." At first this was a hard message for the prosperous Dutch settlers, but within six years the seeds of revival began to grow throughout the Raritan Valley. In 1727, as the Great Moravian Revival was breaking out in Herrnhut, Germany, [2] a spiritual awakening was also beginning in the Raritan Valley congregations, particularly the First Reformed Church in New Brunswick.

The news about revival in Frelinghuysen's church in New Brunswick spread throughout the Colonies, particularly after the Rev. Gilbert Tennent moved to New Brunswick in 1727 and became a prominent revival leader from his pulpit at the First Presbyterian Church.

When George Whitefield spoke in front of Frelinghuysen's church in 1739, more than seven thousand people came to hear this internationally known revival leader describe the Great Awakening that was happening in the Colonies. The audience was amazed at

Whitefield's booming voice and his message of hope for those who came to a saving faith in Jesus Christ. As his voice echoed from the steps of the First Reformed Church down to the bank of the Raritan River—half a mile away—a great tumult of praise erupted from the audience, forcing Whitefield to end his sermon prematurely.

From that day New Brunswick became internationally known as a center of revival. Gilbert Tennent developed a close friendship with Whitefield and traveled with him throughout the Colonies and eventually to England. Like Whitefield, Tennent had a booming voice that projected to thousands of listeners who gathered to hear open-air messages throughout the Colonies.

It is highly appropriate that Gilbert and his brother William are buried at the Old Tennent Church near Freehold, New Jersey. Stones and markers at this church also remind visitors about the price the early settlers paid for their political and religious freedom.

Built by English settlers in 1692, the Old Tennent Church conducted the first Presbyterian worship services in North America. Two generations later, Old Tennent doubled as a military hospital for Continental soldiers during the Revolutionary War. On June 26, 1778, as General Washington was leading his troops to a stalemate against the British Army at the legendary Battle of Monmouth, injured troops were taken to Old Tennent for medical care. Bloodstains from these injured soldiers can still be seen on the lacquered pews of this historic church.

Stones of Remembrance

The Old Testament tells us that one of God's names is Elohim, which is Hebrew for "the God who cuts covenant."[3] The name Elohim indicates that we have a God who remembers His people and keeps covenants with them forever. We can be assured that God remembers every minister, soldier, and settler who ever visited the Old Tennent Church, many of whom became martyrs for their God and country. Just as historians and church leaders have placed hundreds of historical markers across New Jersey to help us remember significant events from the past, God has also instructed us to gather "stones of remembrance" to remind believers in current and coming generations about His mighty deeds.

After the Lord miraculously cut off the Jordan River's floodwaters so the Israelites could walk into the Promised Land, He told Joshua to erect a monument to commemorate this miraculous event. In Joshua 4:2–3 we read God's instructions to the Israelites' leader:

> *"Choose twelve men from among the people, one from each tribe, and tell them to take up twelve stones from the middle of the Jordan from right where the priests stood and to carry them over with you and put them down at the place where you stay tonight."*

Joshua conveys God's further instructions in verses 6–7:

> *"In the future, when your children ask you, 'What do these stones mean?' tell them that the flow of the Jordan was cut off before the ark of the covenant of the LORD. When it crossed the Jordan, the waters of the Jordan were cut off. These stones are to be a memorial to the people of Israel forever."*

Later in this chapter we read that Joshua obeyed God's directive concerning this memorial marker at their camp at Gilgal. In verses 21–24 he tells the twelve tribes to remind their descendants about God's mighty deeds in the past:

> *He said to the Israelites, "In the future when your descendants ask their fathers, 'What do these stones mean?' tell them, 'Israel crossed the Jordan on dry ground.' For the LORD your God dried up the Jordan before you until you had crossed over. The LORD your God did to the Jordan just what he had done to the Red Sea*

when he dried it up before us until we had crossed over. He did this
so that all the peoples of the earth might know that the hand of
the LORD *is powerful and so that you might always fear the* LORD
your God."[4]

The Lord knows that His people have short memories about historical events, and so He provides the written Word as well as "stones of remembrance" to remind us about His great love for mankind and His wondrous deeds in past generations.

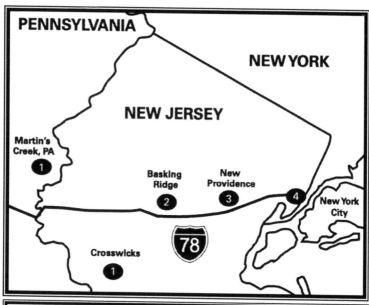

Interstate 78—Highway of Holiness
1. **Martins Creek, PA** (1st Great Awakening)
   Crosswicks, NJ (1st Great Awakening)
2. **Basking Ridge, NJ** (1st Great Awakening)
3. **New Providence, NJ** (2nd Great Awakening)
4. **New York City** (3rd Great Awakening)

Wells of Revival

One day, as I was driving to work along Interstate 78 in New Jersey, I began to realize that many of the exit signs along this road also represented "stones of remembrance." Some of the cities and towns along this road had been scenes of great revivals during the First Great Awakening—Newark, Elizabeth, Basking Ridge, Somerville, and Lamington. Several of the cities and towns experienced revivals in subsequent spiritual awakenings—New Providence, Berkeley Heights, Warrenville, Bernardsville, and Clinton. Other cities remind us of important Revolutionary War battles and outposts—Springfield, Newark, Elizabeth, Basking Ridge, and Morristown. And two communities along this road—Asbury and Cokesbury—were named for prominent Methodist revival leaders who dedicated churches there in the 19th century.

These exit signs prompted me to recall that God has established at least fourteen "wells of revival" along the sixty-mile stretch of I-78 that lies between Easton, Pennsylvania, and New York City.[5] These fourteen wells are listed in Appendix D.

The concept of "wells of revival" is based on Genesis 26:18 and has been described by numerous Christian writers, including Dr. Martyn Lloyd-Jones,[6] George H. Morrison,[7] and Lou Engle.[8] Just as Isaac needed to redig the wells originally dug by his father Abraham, those

> **Those who are interested in seeing a fresh move of spiritual renewal must return to the ancient wells of revival in their area.**

who are interested in seeing a fresh move of spiritual renewal in the 21st century must return to the ancient wells of revival in their area. And just as Isaac's men needed to remove the dirt the Philistines had used to stop up the ancient wells, the church today should study the past in order to determine how these old wells of revival got plugged up. *If we are serious about seeking a new time of refreshment in our church, city, or nation, then we would do well to examine both the* **origins** *of past spiritual awakenings and the historical events that occurred at the* **endings** *of these awakenings.*

Now some readers may wonder what practical benefit can come from studying the history of past revivals. After all, they may say that social, political, and economic conditions have changed drastically in the past century. While we may be interested, for example, in knowing that God brought revival to the nation of Wales in 1904–05, what reason do we have to believe that He intends to bring a fresh wave of revival to that country a hundred years later?

My response to this potential objection is fourfold. First, every historical revival is God's response to the fervent prayers of His people. As Matthew Henry once noted, "When God intends great mercy for His people, the first thing He does is set them a-praying."[9] During every period of revival, prayers are answered more quickly and more powerfully than usual. Nevertheless, it is normally the case that many prayer requests remain unanswered at the time the revival ends.

But none of these prayers is ever forgotten or wasted in God's economy of prayer. To the contrary, Revelation 5:8 tells us that the prayers of the saints are stored up in heaven in "golden bowls full of incense." When we pray in agreement with the unanswered prayer requests of past generations, should we not expect that God's heart will be moved, just as it is today when "two of you on earth agree about anything you ask for" (Matthew 18:19)?

Second, as we will show in subsequent chapters, reviewing accounts of past revivals frequently reveals important information about the spiritual dynamics that were operating at that time in history and could apply to the present day. More specifically, in

Chapter Two we will consider what Revelation 1:4 describes as the "seven spirits" or "sevenfold Spirit" standing before the throne of God and how these seven spirits operate during revivals.

Third, while it is certainly true that social, political, and economic circumstances have changed drastically over time, nevertheless God's heart toward His people has not changed. Who would argue, for example, that God's love for New England is any less than it was during the First Great Awakening? *Indeed, what has changed since the First Great Awakening is man's passion for God, not God's passion for man.* As in Joshua's time, God continues to provide "stones of remembrance" so that the present generation "might always fear the LORD your God." As this happens, God's constant hope is that His people will give up their sinful ways. When this occurs, God's promise in 2 Chronicles 7:14 is that He will "hear from heaven and will forgive their sin and will heal their land." We will discuss the concept of healing the land in greater detail in Chapter Ten.

And fourth, the story of Isaac redigging his father's wells gives us hope that God will honor our faithfulness in redigging wells of revival. Genesis 26:32 tells us that after Isaac had unstopped all of Abraham's ancient wells, his servants went on to discover fresh wells of water at Beersheba and other places. This fact should be a great encouragement for all who desire a new outpouring of the Holy Spirit in our time. As we pray to tap into the ancient reservoirs of revival, Genesis 26:32 provides hope that God will show us where to dig for hidden rivers of Holy Spirit power that will refresh men and women in this present generation.

PRAYER

Father, we cry out because the ancient wells of revival have been stopped up in this region. We ask forgiveness for our sinful thoughts, deeds, and attitudes that continue to block the river of life that is flowing beneath the land you have provided for us. Give us eyes to see and ears to hear what you are telling us about how these wells have become clogged, so that we might repent for our sins and for those of our forefathers. Amen.

The Spirit of the Lord and Revival

Three Types of Revivals

As I reflected about past spiritual awakenings in the United States, I realized that Isaiah 11:2 contains a profound insight about the works of the Holy Spirit in revival. In the NIV translation this verse states,

> The Spirit of the LORD will rest on him—
> the Spirit of wisdom and of understanding,
> the Spirit of counsel and of power,
> the Spirit of knowledge and of the fear of the LORD.

This verse explicitly refers to not one but seven spirits (or "sevenfold Spirit")—analogous to the references to the seven eyes of Christ (Revelation 5:6), the seven golden lampstands, seven churches, and seven angels described in the book of Revelation (1:4, 1:20) as well as to the seven "redemptive gifts" Paul mentions in Romans 12:6–8.[1]

In an audiotape message about revival, Canadian evangelist Todd Bentley notes that the Bible frequently links together wisdom and understanding, counsel and power, and knowledge and fear of the Lord.[2] It occurred to me that this concept helps explain why

27

there have been very different patterns of revival in different periods of American history.

In the First Great Awakening, for example, Pastor Jonathan Edwards would frequently give an extended sermon on a great doctrine such as salvation, justification, or the glory of God, and then proceed to tell his congregation about the impending judgment that will occur when God's wrath is poured out over unrepentant humanity. In **Thoughts on the Revival,** for example, he wrote,

> *Extraordinary views of divine things, and the religious affections, were frequently attended with very great effects on the body. . . . This quiet rejoicing has been with trembling, i.e., attended with a deep and lively sense of the greatness and majesty of God, and the person's own exceeding littleness and vileness. . . . These things already mentioned have been attended also with the following things, viz.: An extraordinary sense of the awful majesty, great-ness, and holiness of God, so as sometimes to overwhelm soul and body; a sense of the piercing all-seeing eye of God, so as sometimes to take away the bodily strength; and an extraordinary view of the infinite terribleness of the wrath of God; together with a sense of the ineffable misery of sinners who are exposed to this wrath. . . . A sight of the fullness and glorious sufficiency of Christ, has been so affecting as to overcome the body.*[3]

In short, Edwards linked together knowledge of the King-dom of God and the need to walk in the fear of the Lord.

In the Second Great Awakening (1792–1820), the New Divini-ty preachers in Connecticut faithfully followed Edwards' methods and saw revival come to fifty to sixty communities between 1797 and 1799.[4] In the detailed accounts originally published in the **Connecticut Evangelical Magazine,** it is clear that this same pattern of biblical teaching and invoking the fear of the Lord led thousands of men and women to Christ during that awakening.[5]

Most of the revival leaders during that awakening had studied at Yale University under men such as Timothy Dwight, Samuel Hopkins, and Joseph Bellamy—all of whom were intimately familiar with Edwards' accounts of the awakenings that occurred in his Northampton, Massachusetts, and surrounding communities.

But then a very different type of revival broke out in Cane Ridge, Kentucky, in 1801. According to eyewitness accounts from that awakening, there were dozens or even hundreds of extemporaneous sermons by people from all walks of life—including teenagers with no formal theological training. Someone would stand up on a stump, begin exhorting the crowd, and soon a large group of people would come to saving faith and demonstrate a wide variety of physical manifestations, including falling to the ground, speaking in tongues, and so on.[6] Reformed commentators such as Iain Murray[7] have explained this phenomenon as a product of the lack of proper seminary training on the Kentucky frontier, in contrast to the more traditional revival accounts coming out of the Connecticut revivals during the same years.

Following the Cane Ridge awakening, revival leaders such as Charles G. Finney began to develop a style of revival meeting that was subsequently adopted in Methodist camp meetings, in the Welsh Revival of 1904, and in most of the Pentecostal and charismatic revivals of the 20th century. These latter awakenings have typically involved leaders who exhorted their listeners to come to Christ and have involved manifestations of the "charismatic" gifts Paul lists in 1 Corinthians 12:8–11.

Is it possible that God has also chosen a second method of revival based on "the Spirit of counsel and of power"?

Then a different type of revival began in New York City in 1857. In that awakening God raised up a businessman—Jeremiah Lanphier—who began a series of noontime prayer meetings. With no preaching and a minimum of publicity, these noon meetings quickly grew to 10,000 men and women daily by the winter of 1858. There was no doctrinal preaching, no exhortation to "get right with Jesus Christ," and no fanfare whatsoever, but the so-called "Businessman's Revival" (or "Layman's Revival") quickly spread across the U.S. and around the world. In two years approximately five percent of the population of the United States came to Jesus Christ through these meetings conducted by business leaders.[8]

Did God begin to use a third type of revival at that time— one based on "the Spirit of wisdom and understanding"?

We can summarize these observations in Table 1:

Table 1: Three Types of Revivals

Type of Revival	Spiritual Operations
I	**Wisdom and Understanding**
II	**Counsel and Power**
III	**Knowledge and Fear of the Lord**

If these observations are correct, they have significant implications for those who are praying for a new wave of revival in their church, city, or nation. If God's principal method of bringing revival to an area in the past has been through Knowledge and Fear of the Lord (Type III in the table above), then an appropriate strategy for "redigging the wells of revival"[9] is to pray for the Lord to send an outpouring of Knowledge and Fear of the Lord once again! And similarly for Type I and Type II revivals.

Jonathan Edwards' God-Entranced Worldview

In October 2003 more than 2,500 people gathered in Minneapolis to celebrate the 300th anniversary of the birthday of Jonathan Edwards. The overall theme of the conference was "A God-Entranced Vision of All Things: The Unrivaled Legacy of Jonathan Edwards." John Piper and Justin Taylor subsequently published an edited volume of messages from the conference.[10] The consensus that emerged from this gathering is that not only was Edwards arguably the most gifted philosopher-theologian who ever lived in the United States, but also his writings have continuing significance for today's evangelical church.

From Piper and Taylor's summary of addresses at this conference, at least five aspects of Edwards' life and ministry are significant for us today:

1. **PERSPECTIVE**
2. **PURPOSE**
3. **PRAISE**
4. **PASSION** and
5. **PRAYER**

Let's briefly consider each of these aspects.

1. PERSPECTIVE

Pastor John Piper, who organized the conference, states that the church today needs to rediscover Edwards' theocentric worldview. In the subsequent book based on this conference's addresses, he concludes,

> *What is missing [in the evangelical church today] is the mind-shaping knowledge and the all-transforming enjoyment of the weight of the glory of God. The glory of God—holy, righteous,*

all-wise, all-good—is missing. God rests lightly on the church in America. He is not felt as a weighty concern.[11]

So what was Edwards' worldview? Piper provides the following summary statement from Edwards' monograph, "The Dissertation Concerning the End for Which God Created the World":

*All that is ever spoken of in the Scripture as an ultimate end of God's works is included in that one phrase, **the glory of God.** . . . The refulgence shines upon and into the creature, and is reflected back to the luminary. The beams of glory come from God, and are something of God and are refunded back again to their original. So that the whole is **of** God, and **in** God, and **to** God, and God is the beginning, middle and end in this affair.*[12]

Edwards conceived of God as being absolutely sovereign, self-sufficient in Himself, infinite in holiness, and perfectly glorious. Furthermore, since God has no deficiencies, everything He does is motivated by the passion to express and display His glorious sufficiency. This being the case, the believer's duty and privilege is to reflect the value of God's glory in everything we think and do.

It is worthwhile to consider why this "God-entranced worldview" is so foreign to 21st century Christians. Conference speaker Dr. J. I. Packer noted that Edwards' agenda in studying religion was God's divine plan for creation, not religious psychology. He claims that today's human-centered culture has difficulty in conceiving what the Puritans and Reformed teachers focused on in the 17th and 18th centuries. He writes,

Living as we do in a human-centered culture shaped by the Enlightenment, and surrounded as we are by human-centered forms of religion in as well as outside the churches, following Edwards at this point calls us to an effort of rethinking, reimagining, recentering our attention, reeducating our desires, and refocusing our affections that is almost beyond our strength. Evangelical and liberal theology are, to be sure, always and necessarily at logger-heads, because cognitive revelation, on which evangelicalism builds, and cognitive relativism, which is basic to liberalism, are totally antithetical.

But for two centuries now evangelical and liberal pietists have been joining hands to give a personal religion, previously defined as knowledge and service to God, a subjective twist that effectively defines it as the experience of reaching after, and trying to main-tain, some knowledge and service of God amid the ups and downs and strains and pains of daily life. The reference-point has moved; the study of religion— professedly Christian religion, that is—has become a study of human feelings, atti-tudes, and struggles rather than of God's

> **Our first challenge is to look at our present condi-tion from God's point of view rather than from our own human perspective.**

gifts and calling and works and ways with humans, which was Edwards' agenda. Edwards has, indeed, an unquenchable interest in Christian and pseudo-Christian religious experience, which he describes and dissects with great clinical skill; but his interest is theocentric rather than anthropocentric, intellectual rather than sentimental, theological rather than anthropological, and doxo-logical rather than psychological. . . . What a downslide there has been![13]

Piper and other leading evangelical theologians lament that alt-hough Edwards' piety and theology continued on in academic Calvinistic circles, "there were no successors to his God-entranced world view."[14] Our first challenge, then, is to look at our present condition from God's point of view rather than from our own human perspective.

This problem of perspective is exactly what the Apostle John writes about in Revelation 5:1–6. In his prophetic vision of the scroll with seven seals, he first grieved that no one was able to open the seals. Then he looked up and saw the Lion of the tribe of Judah, who was worthy to perform this task (v. 5). As he continued to look upward toward heaven, he saw that the Lion of Judah now appeared to him as a Lamb that was slain (v. 6). The same Being that looked like a Lion from below became a Lamb when John observed Him from a higher perspective! He then provided numerous details about how the elders as well as "many angels, numbering thousands upon thousands" encircled the throne and began worshiping the Lamb who was slain.

This scripture passage reminds us that the problems we face have both temporal and eternal dimensions. If we view our circumstances from a temporal perspective, they often seem much larger than we are. We become like the ten spies who reported to Moses that their enemy was huge: "We seemed like grasshoppers in our own eyes, and we looked the same to them" (Numbers 13:33). But Caleb and Joshua disagreed, saying, "We should go up and take possession of the land, for we can certainly do it" (Numbers 13:30).

When we focus on our worldly problems, they often appear overwhelming. Our enemies look like giants, and Jesus appears to us as a roaring lion. But when we exercise prayer, worship, and other spiritual disciplines to raise our perspective to God's level, our problems start to shrink in comparison. As we ascend on God's "high-way," the giants we face begin to appear as grasshoppers. At the same time we begin to see Jesus as the meek and lowly Lamb who was slain and who wants to take all of our earthly burdens from us. Just as Isaiah discovered that God's "highway" was the path to Zion (Isaiah 35:8–10), we also must rise above our cultural worldview to attain a God-centered perspective on our lives and situations. We will explore the concept of a spiritual highway in subsequent chapters.

2. PURPOSE

The purpose of man is a second key aspect of Edwards' life and ministry that was described at the Minneapolis conference. Piper explains that Edwards was totally in agreement with the Westminster Catechism, which stated that man's chief end is to glorify God and to enjoy Him forever. But Edwards has a lot more to say about this matter:

> *The enjoyment of God is the only happiness with which our souls can be satisfied. To go to heaven, fully to enjoy God, is infinitely better than the most pleasant accommodations here. Fathers and mothers, husbands, wives, or children, or the company of earthly friends, are but shadows; but God is the substance. These are but scattered beams, but God is the sun. These are but streams. But God is the ocean.* **Therefore it becomes us to spend this life only as a journey toward heaven, as it becomes us to make the seeking of our highest end and proper good, the whole work of our lives; to which we should subordinate all other concerns of this life.** *Why should we labour for, or set our hearts on, any thing else, but that which is our proper end, and true happiness?*[15] [emphasis added]

This statement about the purpose of man, as well as the perspective mentioned above, is not an original idea in Jonathan Edwards' theology. On the contrary, they amplify themes presented in scripture verses such as Matthew 22:37 ("Love the Lord [our] God with all [our] heart and with all [our] soul and with all [our] mind") and Romans 11:36 ("[All things are] from him and through him and to him. . . . To him be the glory forever!"). But Piper,

Packer, and other writers agree that Edwards was gifted to articulate this vision better than other writers in the evangelical tradition.

3. PRAISE

A third key aspect of Edwards' life and ministry was his lifelong emphasis on praising God. Based on his observation that God is glorified by His creatures' delight in Him, Jonathan and Sarah Edwards sang hymns and praised God at every available opportunity. Piper provides the following quotation about Edwards' view of praise:

> **God is glorified not only by His glory's being seen, but by its being rejoiced in.** *When those that see it delight in it, God is more glorified than if they only see it. His glory is then received by the whole soul, both by the understanding and by the heart. God made the world that He might communicate, and the creature receive, His glory; and that it might [be] received both by the mind and heart. He that testifies his idea of God's glory [doesn't] glorify God so much as he that testifies also his . . . delight in it.*[16] [emphasis original]

George Marsden's biography of Edwards amplifies on this theme. He writes,

> *Edwards worked constantly to cultivate gratitude, praise, worship, and dependence on his Savior. Whatever his failings, he attempted every day to see Christ's love in all things, to walk according to God's precepts, and to give up attachments to worldly pleasures in anticipation of that closer spiritual union that death would bring.*[17]

4. PASSION

A fourth notable aspect of Edwards' life and ministry was his great passion for Christ. During his years at Yale College he began penning a series of Resolutions, which he continually added to and followed throughout his adult life. At the Minneapolis conference J. I. Packer noted that Edwards was described as "God-centered, God-focused, God-intoxicated, and God-entranced."[18]

During his lifetime Edwards wrote more than seventy Resolutions, which are published in his *Memoirs* and several other sources. A glance at the following examples will show how serious he was about living a strict, disciplined life that was glorifying to God:

1. Resolved, *that I will do whatsoever I think to be most to God's glory, and my own good, profit and pleasure, in the whole of my duration, without any consideration of the time, whether now, or never so many myriads of ages hence. Resolved to do whatever I think to be my duty and most for the good and advantage of mankind in general. Resolved to do this, whatever difficulties I meet with, how many soever, and how great soever.*

2. Resolved, *never to lose one moment of time; but to improve it the most profitable way I possibly can.*

3. Resolved, *never to do anything, which I should be afraid to do, if it were the last hour of my life.*

4. Resolved, *never to speak evil of anyone, so that it shall tend to his dishonor, more or less, upon no account except for some real good.*

5. Resolved, *to endeavor to obtain for myself as much happiness, in the other world, as I possibly can, with all the power, might, vigor, and vehemence, yea violence, I am capable of, or can bring myself to exert, in any way that can be thought of.*

6.   Resolved, *to study the Scriptures so steadily, constantly and frequently, as that I may find, and plainly perceive myself to grow in the knowledge of the same.*

7.   Resolved, *never to count that a prayer, nor to let that pass as a prayer, nor that as a petition of a prayer, which is so made, that I cannot hope that God will answer it; nor that as a confession, which I cannot hope God will accept.*

8.   Resolved, *to strive to my utmost every week to be brought higher in religion, and to a higher exercise of grace, than I was the week before.*

9.   Resolved, *to do always, what I can towards making, maintaining, and preserving peace, when it can be done without overbalancing detriment to other respects.*

10. Resolved, *to inquire every night, as I am going to bed, wherein I have been negligent, what sin I have committed, and wherein I have denied myself; also at the end of every week, month and year.*[19]

5.   *PRAYER*

A fifth key aspect of Edwards' life and ministry noted by speakers at the 2003 Jonathan Edwards conference in Minneapolis was his lifelong commitment to prayer. Speaker Donald Whitney writes,

> *Edwards was so devoted to prayer that it is hard to find a daily routine for him that wasn't permeated with it. He prayed alone when he arose, then had family prayer before breakfast. Prayer was a part of each meal, and he prayed again with the family in the evening. He prayed over his studies, and he prayed as he walked in the evenings. Prayer was both a discipline and a part of his leisure.*[20]

In 1747 Edwards wrote a major treatise on the subject of "concerts of prayer." The title of this treatise is quite descriptive: ***An Humble Attempt to Promote Explicit Agreement and Visible Union Among God's People, in Extraordinary Prayer for the Revival of Religion, and the Advancement of Christ's Kingdom on Earth, Pursuant to Scripture Promises and Prophecies Concerning the Last Time.*** This work had two explicit goals: (1) to promote prayer for the revival of the Christian church (as the primary agency through which Christ manifests His glory on earth) and (2) to encourage the church, once revived, to be active with God's Spirit in the advancement of God's Kingdom throughout the world.[21]

Edwards was constantly looking for "hopeful signs" of the advancement of the Kingdom of God through spiritual awakenings and other means, although he did not expect Christ to return to earth until after the year 2000.[22] Before Christ's return, however, he believed that it was the church's duty to prepare humankind for His second coming:

> The world is made for the Son of God; his kingdom is the **end** of all changes that come to pass in the state of the world. All are only to prepare the way for this.[23]

How Can I Gain a God-Entranced Worldview?

In his authoritative biography ***Jonathan Edwards: A Life***, George Marsden describes how the Holy Spirit allowed Edwards to overcome his rebellion against God in March of 1722:

> His reason and his moral sensibilities had put a huge obstacle in his path. These objections were manifestations of a rebelliousness against the orthodoxy of his parents, dating to childhood. He could not believe in God's total sovereignty, the doctrine at the

very foundation of Calvinist teaching. Yet he was also sure that he had no hope on his own. . . . He desperately wanted to trust in God, yet he could not believe in, let alone be subject to, such a tyrant.

In the midst of this turmoil, he had a breakthrough. Suddenly he became convinced that indeed God was just in "eternally disposing of men, according to his sovereign pleasure." The tortuous obstacle was removed. . . .

This intellectual breakthrough later seemed the work of the Holy Spirit because it soon had an overwhelming spiritual manifestation. At first Jonathan's mind simply "rested" in his insights, "and it put an end to all those cavils and objections, that I had till then abode with me, all the preceding part of my life." Then one day came a wondrous response, far beyond what his intellect could produce. He was reading 1 Timothy 1:17, "Now unto the King eternal, invisible, the only wise God, be honor and glory forever and ever, Amen." He had heard these words countless times and long since repeated catechism answers cataloguing such attributions of the deity and emphasizing that people existed to "glorify and enjoy" (or be in a state of joy with) God. Now the implications of the incomprehensible greatness of the God of the vast universe who was truly eternal and all wise flamed out at him. As he read these words, he recalled, "there came into my soul, and was as it were diffused through it, a sense of the glory of the divine being; a new sense, quite different from anything I ever experienced before." He was so much enraptured that, as he put it, "I thought with myself, how excellent a Being that was; and how happy I should be, if I might enjoy that God, and be wrapped up to God in heaven, and be as it were swallowed up in him." He kept repeating the verse "and as it were singing over these words of Scripture to myself . . . and prayed in a manner quite different from what I used to do; with a new sort of affection."[24]

Marsden continues by describing another divine encounter that Edwards had later that year:

> *He was at home for vacation in the spring and had been talking to his father about what was happening. Jonathan recalled that he was "pretty much affected" by this conversation, and when it ended he walked alone in the fields for contemplation. "And as I was walking there," he reported, "and looked up on the sky and clouds; there came into my mind, a sweet sense of the glorious majesty and grace of God, that I know not how to express." What overwhelmed him was two seemingly opposite attributes of the triune God "in a sweet conjunction: majesty and meekness joined together: it was a sweet and gentle, and holy majesty; and also a majestic meekness; an awful sweetness; a high, and great, and holy gentleness."*[25]

As the result of these and other encounters, Edwards attained the God-entranced worldview that we have already discussed above. Marsden summarizes this shift in his thinking as follows:

> *In fact, it was only when Jonathan's vision expanded to appreciate that the triune God who controlled this vast universe must be ineffably good, beautiful, and loving beyond human comprehension that he could lose himself in God.*[26]

So what can we learn from these passages? Should we dismiss these extraordinary encounters as interesting but irrelevant anecdotes for 21st century Christian life? Or should we go to the opposite extreme and expect that God will give us the same ecstatic experiences that Edwards had as a youth? Let me suggest a middle course of action that is based on the following observations: (1) Edwards' rebelliousness stemmed from being deceived by the god of this age; (2) the breakthrough occurred when the power of the Holy Spirit destroyed the enemy's hold over his life; and (3) Edwards received his God-entranced worldview as he continually meditated over the excellencies of God and allowed this concept to change his heart.

In regard to the first point, the Apostle Paul tells us in 2 Corinthians 4:3–4 that

> [E]ven if our gospel is veiled, it is veiled to those who are perishing. The god of this age has blinded the minds of unbelievers, so that they cannot see the light of the gospel of the glory of Christ, who is the image of God.

Moreover, Paul indicates in Galatians 3:1 that spiritual deception can occur even within the Body of Christ:

> You foolish Galatians! Who has bewitched you? Before your very eyes Jesus Christ was clearly portrayed as crucified.

We do not know for sure whether "the god of this age" refers to Satan himself or to other idols such as materialism, power, or lust. But these scripture passages should convince us that our rebelliousness is caused by the same dark powers that caused Edwards to be spiritually blinded until his breakthrough in 1722.

Second, we will not escape from blindness unless this same Holy Spirit does a miraculous work of grace in our mind and heart. As much as Edwards loved philosophy and logic, he realized that the decisive factor in his spiritual breakthrough was a work of pure grace, not his own intellectual achievement. He understood well that his conversion was totally the work of God through the Holy Spirit. He acknowledged that his own human reason was insufficient to bridge the gap between the righteousness and sovereignty of God and his own sinfulness. This is a theme he later expounded eloquently in his classic book **Religious Affections.**

Using modern terminology, what Edwards received from the Holy Spirit was an impartation of power that allowed him to engage in spiritual warfare against demonic strongholds. As he prayed to

God and meditated over 1 Timothy 1:17 and other scripture verses, he was using the weapons of warfare that Paul describes in 2 Corinthians 10:4–5:

> *The weapons we fight with are not the weapons of the world. On the contrary, they have divine power to demolish strongholds. We demolish arguments and every pretension that sets itself up against the knowledge of God, and we take captive every thought to make it obedient to Christ.*

Third, as Edwards continued to meditate on the excellencies of God, both his worldview and his heart experienced the transformation that Paul describes in Romans 12:1–2:

> *Therefore, I urge you, brothers, in view of God's mercy, to offer your bodies as living sacrifices, holy and pleasing to God—this is your spiritual act of worship. Do not conform any longer to the pattern of this world, but be transformed by the renewing of your mind. Then you will be able to test and approve what God's will is—his good, pleasing and perfect will.*

Based on these three observations, **I believe that each one of us has the potential to gain the God-entranced worldview that Jonathan Edwards had.** Although none of us is likely to have the same experiences that he did, the same Holy Spirit is available today to transform our lives as well as our perspective on the Kingdom of God.

Moreover, the Bible teaches that the same spiritual principles that transform our lives are also applicable to transforming the spiritual climate in cities and nations. When Jesus gathered the seventy-two leaders, as described in Luke 10, He gave them very specific instructions about how to reach the lost. Today we refer to this model as Prayer Evangelism.

Gravestone at Mt. Bethel Meetinghouse in Warrenville, New Jersey. This was the site of numerous Baptist awakenings during the 19ᵗʰ century.

How Prayer Evangelism Changes the Spiritual Climate

According to Ed Silvoso, the essence of Prayer Evangelism is "talking to God about our neighbors before we talk to our neighbors about God."[27] In Luke 10 Jesus instructs His followers to do four things as they went ahead of Him into many towns and places where He was about to go:

1. Speak peace to them.

2. Fellowship with them.

3. Take care of their needs.

4. Proclaim the good news.

These four instructions are contained in verses 5, 8, and 9:

"When you enter a house, first say, 'Peace to this house.'. . . When you enter a town and are welcomed, eat what is set before you. Heal the sick who are there and tell them, 'The kingdom of God is near you.'"

Prayer Evangelism asserts that these four steps must be done in the proper sequence:

The first of these four steps will open the door to the second step and so forth. It is very important for us to understand that the steps are interconnected and, to be effective, must be implemented in the order given. . . .

This four-step method proved so successful that soon after Jesus taught it to His disciples, multitudes came to believe in Jesus and demons surrendered en masse to a bunch of rookie evangelists. Unfortunately, these are not the results we see today when we evangelize. What is the problem? Rather than following Jesus' four-step

> **Prayer Evangelism is a key strategy to break strongholds and to change the spiritual climate in cities and nations.**

approach, we reverse the order and begin with the last step, witnessing, and skip the blessing, the fellowship and the caring that are to precede the good news. In most cases, this approach to witnessing does not work.[28]

Ed Silvoso then explains the spiritual principles behind the Prayer Evangelism model. In summary:

• Speaking peace *opens the door to unbiased fellowship with those we meet. As we speak peace, we bless them and disarm feelings of anger that give jurisdiction to the enemy.*

- Fellowshiping with our hosts *establishes a level of trust, which in turn encourages them to express their felt needs to us.*
- Praying for their felt needs *allows us to express our concern for them and to intercede to God on their behalf. This invites the Holy Spirit to come into their lives with demonstrations of the power of God.*
- Teaching the gospel *helps them to understand that the Kingdom of God has come near unto them. We do not take them into the Kingdom; instead, we present the Kingdom to them.*[29]

When the seventy-two went ahead of Jesus and applied these principles, they ministered with surprising effectiveness. They reported that "even the demons submit to us in your name" (Luke 10:17). Jesus confirmed their report by replying that "I saw Satan fall like lightning from heaven" (Luke 10:18). He then thanked the Father for revealing these principles to "little children" rather than to "the wise and learned" (Luke 10:21). Glory be to God for revealing these principles of spiritual renewal to us—not only for our individual lives but also for cities and nations!

Summary

In this chapter we have seen that several waves of revival have occurred in the United States and, in particular, in New Jersey. These waves not only occurred at different times and places but also demonstrated different types of spiritual operations. Based on the insights we gained from Isaiah 11:2, it seems reasonable to believe that many of the variations between revivals are due to the different spiritual operations in effect. For simplicity Table 1 summarized these spiritual operations as three types of revivals: (1) revivals based on Wisdom and Understanding (Type I), (2) revivals based on Counsel and Power (Type II), and (3) revivals based on Knowledge and Fear of the Lord (Type III).

We also reviewed the concepts of a "God-entranced vision of all things," which was prominent in the evangelical church during the First and Second Great Awakenings; and the idea of a spiritual "highway." We then looked at how the enemy has blinded the eyes of nonbelievers as well as believers. Unless the Holy Spirit performs a miraculous work in our lives, we can easily be misled by "the god of this age" and misinterpret important scriptures.

Finally, we provided a brief summary of Prayer Evangelism and described why it is a key strategy to break down spiritual strongholds in our personal lives and to change the spiritual climate in a city or even a nation. *Let's keep these ideas in mind as we begin our journey along my Highway of Holiness.*

PRAYER

Father, I ask that you would pour out your Spirit upon me, that I might be anointed to proclaim the Good News of Jesus Christ to the poor, the prisoners, the oppressed, and those who have physical or emotional infirmities. I pray that you would allow me to be an instrument of renewal and revival in my home, neighborhood, congregation, marketplace, and nation. Grant that I might also receive the fullness of the Holy Spirit as I use my spiritual gifts to advance your Kingdom on earth today. In Jesus' precious name I pray. Amen.

CHAPTER THREE

My Highway of Holiness

Can These Accounts Be True?

One day in early 1999 I stopped at a local Christian bookstore to purchase some materials for my adult education class at the Presbyterian Church at New Providence, New Jersey. As I walked past the rack of new books at the front of the bookstore, one title caught my attention. It was a documentary entitled *The Rising Revival,* edited by Drs. C. Peter Wagner and Pablo Deiros.[1] "A strange title," I thought to myself. I had heard about revivals in Pensacola, Florida; Toronto, and other places, but I couldn't imagine how these movements had anything to do with the present state of the evangelical Christian community in New Jersey.

I took another look at the book and was intrigued by the subtitle: *Firsthand Accounts of the Incredible Argentine Revival— and How It Can Spread Throughout the World.* I decided to pull the book off the rack to see what kinds of accounts they were talking about. I must confess that I had never heard of either of the editors, and I was more than a bit skeptical that this was just another hyped book delivering little substance.

A quick perusal of the inside book jacket, however, caused me to check my initial reaction. Here were two Ph.D.'s, one from the

United States and the other from Argentina, who had collected documentary accounts about a nationwide spiritual awakening that had been going on, non-stop, for nearly two decades. The book included eyewitness reports, by a dozen writers, about events that sounded like stories taken from the book of Acts. For example, since 1982 one marketplace leader (Carlos Annacondia) had been conducting evangelical campaigns in which nearly 2 million people had accepted Jesus as their Lord and Savior.

Another chapter told about a prison church formed inside Argentina's largest maximum security prison in the 1980s. Now, fifteen years later, the author (Rev. Juan Zuccarelli) claimed that more than three thousand inmates in that prison had received Christ into their lives. Another chapter in the book described a church in Buenos Aires that had documented more than 10,000 physical healings since the beginning of the revival in 1982. And two other chapters gave accounts about how two entire cities (Resistencia and Adrogué) were being reached for Christ through the ministry of Harvest Evangelism. "Can these accounts be true?" I asked myself.

By now I'd decided to purchase the book. I thought, "Either this book is a total fraud, or else I need to broaden my conceptions about how God operates in revivals today." That evening I picked up **The Rising Revival** and prayed that the Holy Spirit would speak to me about the topic of revivals. In the years since my parents' trip to New Jersey described in Chapter One, I had read several historical accounts about New Jersey towns that had experienced revivals in the past—Newark, Elizabeth, Basking Ridge, Freehold, Woodbridge, and several others. But all of these accounts came from the 18th and 19th centuries, and there seemed to be little evidence of spiritual awakening in any of these towns at present— none, at least, significant enough to make the local news media. Besides, the events described in **The Rising Revival** seemed to be entirely different from the accounts I had read about the First and Second Great Awakenings.

Then the words of Jesus came to me from John 16:13–15:

"But when he, the Spirit of truth, comes, he will guide you into all truth. He will not speak on his own; he will speak only what he hears, and he will tell you what is yet to come. He will bring glory to me by taking from what is mine and making it known to you. All that belongs to the Father is mine. That is why I said the Spirit will take from what is mine and make it known to you."

"That's it," I thought as I reflected on what I had just read about the revival in Argentina. "There are probably some parts of these accounts that are true, and other parts that have been overstated," I said to myself. I felt that I had just received a new historical research assignment from the Holy Spirit! I gladly accepted this assignment, confident that the Holy Spirit would honor the promise to lead me into all truth. If any part of the Argentine revival was a genuine work of God, I wanted the Holy Spirit to take that which was of God and make it known to me.

Preparing the Way Conference

My father went to be with the Lord in the spring of 1999. My parents had purchased a small cemetery plot in Dad's hometown in southeast Iowa. As I flew in to Cedar Rapids the day before his burial, I reflected about how good the Lord had been to my family. Dad had worked his way through college by shoveling coal and by monitoring chapel attendance at Coe College, which was very strict about enforcing chapel participation at that time. He didn't like the task of reporting classmates who had cut chapel worship, but scholarship money and jobs were scarce during the Great Depression. Dad was also an outstanding tennis player. He served as captain of his college tennis team during his senior year (1936) and was the Cedar Rapids men's tennis champion that year.

I also thought quite a bit about my childhood in Burlington, Iowa, especially about the First Presbyterian Church, which my family attended while living in Burlington. It was a very traditional congregation, and I became a member there during my junior high school years. I have been a member of Presbyterian churches since then, except for a period when I worshiped at a United Church of Christ congregation during college.

Since Dad's burial was scheduled for the day before Easter, my wife, Joanne, and I decided to spend Easter Sunday in Cedar Rapids. The Cedar Rapids *Gazette* announced that a special Passion Play was being held every night that week at the First Assembly of God, and we thought it would be encouraging to attend their Saturday night performance after Dad's burial service and dinner with family members.

The Passion Play was an extraordinary "love offering" from the First Assembly of God to the community of Cedar Rapids. More than five hundred church members participated in this pageant, either as actors or as members of the mass choir. It was exactly the refreshment Joanne and I needed after a difficult but joyful "home-coming" for Dad.

The people we met at the Passion Play were very friendly and invited us to come back for their Easter service the next day. Although neither Joanne nor I had ever attended an Assembly of God worship service, we agreed to return the next morning.

When we arrived, Pastor Larry Sohn and his wife greeted us warmly at the door, and we felt instantly at home. The praise music was very uplifting, and I particularly enjoyed Pastor Larry's request for the choir to sing the old hymn, "And Can It Be." That was one of the hymns Joanne and I had picked for our wedding at the New Providence church in 1988.

After the introductory worship music, Pastor Larry asked all the visitors to raise their hands, which we did. Then a member of the congregation handed us a visitors' welcome kit, which included information about the congregation and upcoming events. We enjoyed the sermon and the remainder of the service that day, but I confess that I don't remember the title of the pastor's message or any of his key points.

What I do remember from the service, however, was opening the welcome kit and riveting my eyes on the sheet of upcoming conferences. The schedule listed a revival conference featuring three of the Argentine pastors I had read about in *The Rising Revival.* That Easter Sunday I told Joanne I wanted to return to Cedar Rapids to attend this three-day revival conference in November. I realized that this would be my best opportunity to meet some of these Argentine revival leaders in person.

Joanne's work schedule prevented her from joining me that November, and so I flew out to Cedar Rapids by myself. Three months prior to the conference I had torn a muscle in my right leg while jogging, and so on the first morning of the conference I remember wrapping my injured leg in an elastic bandage to minimize the pain and swelling.

In the first session that morning Pastor Sergio Scataglini from Argentina gave a sermon entitled "Preparing the Way for the Lord," a powerful message on the importance of cultivating personal holiness. After Sergio spoke, another Argentine pastor[2] joined him to pray for physical healing for those attending the conference. A strange, but wonderful, sensation went through my right leg while these pastors prayed, and I realized that my leg had been instantly healed. That was the last day I needed the elastic bandage on my leg. Praise the Lord!

At exactly the same time my leg was healed, a Korean woman standing near me began talking excitedly in her native language.

Her daughter, who was bilingual, nudged my elbow and explained to me that her mother's chronic knee condition had just been healed. I can't begin to tell you everything else that happened at that moment, but the subsequent testimonies I heard indicated that as many as one hundred conferees had received spiritual, physical, and/or emotional healing during that thirty-minute prayer meeting.

After that morning session I called Joanne and told her everything that had happened so far at the conference. We were delighted that my leg had been healed, but we needed several days to process this situation after I returned to New Jersey. We both knew I had experienced a powerful, but brief, encounter with Jehovah Rapha—"the God Who Heals." Now we had the difficult task of understanding what this healing meant and how to explain it to our friends back home. Ultimately we decided to tell the story about the healing of my leg to a few close friends in our Bible study group. Like Mary in Luke 2:19, after her encounter with the shepherds and their awesome testimony from the angels about her child, we "treasured up all these things and pondered them" in our hearts for many days.

In the fall of 2000 I learned that Pastor Scataglini was scheduled to speak again on holiness at the Church on the Move in Allentown, Pennsylvania. I invited some friends from our church and Hispanic friends from the First Presbyterian Church of Dunellen, New Jersey, to attend the conference with me. At Allentown Pastor Sergio repeated his message on preparing the way for the Lord, using his book, *The Fire of His Holiness,* as the text. On the first night he announced that there would be a time of prayer for healing on Friday night, the last day of this conference. Each night I drove from New Jersey to Allentown along Interstate 78, with my Hispanic friends driving in a separate van. During the sixty-mile trip to Allentown on the last night of the conference, I remembered the prayer time for healing at Cedar Rapids the previous year and wondered whether the Holy Spirit would show up in Allentown to usher in another powerful wave of healing.

The Friday healing time, however, was not a repeat of what I had experienced in Cedar Rapids. When Pastor Sergio prayed for personal holiness and healing, many people in the audience were deeply convicted that they needed to repent for their sins. But I don't recall seeing a single person who received physical healing that evening.

Afterwards I remember walking across the parking lot to talk with my Hispanic friends in the other van. I felt particularly sorry for a Colombian man, Javier Echeverry, who had broken his back four and a half years earlier and could walk only with the assistance of a four-post walker. I offered a quick prayer for Javier and my other friends who had come to the conference that night seeking physical healing.

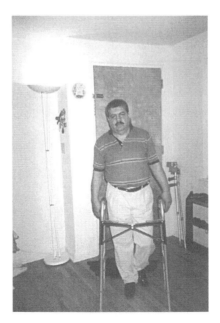

Photo of Javier Echeverry in December 2000

It's God!

In March of 2001 the Church on the Move invited another one of the Argentine revival leaders, Pastor Claudio Freidzon, to lead a Holy Spirit conference at their church in Allentown. I didn't know much about Pastor Claudio but had enjoyed his message about the Argentine revival at the Cedar Rapids conference in 1999.

On Wednesday, the first night of the conference, Pastor Freidzon blessed the pastors from the Lehigh Valley who were in attendance, and gave a rousing message from Isaiah 6 about God's desire to use each believer to advance His Kingdom. He announced that he would conduct an open-ended service on Friday night to lay hands on all who desired prayers for healing.

Many from the Dunellen congregation returned on Thursday to hear Pastor Freidzon remind us of God's promise that "he will command his angels concerning you to guard you in all your ways; they will lift you up in their hands, so that you will not strike your foot against a stone" (Psalm 91:11–12). That night I sat next to Pastor Silvio del Campo and his wife and friends from the Dunellen congregation. We were seated in the middle of the center section, but Javier Echeverry and another friend took less comfortable bleacher seats closer to the altar.

I was greatly encouraged by Pastor Freidzon's message on Thursday and decided to return the following evening. I did not make arrangements to carpool with my friends from Dunellen on Friday, since I knew that they had prior plans to attend their usual Friday night praise service in their own church. What I did not know, however, was that Pastor Silvio had decided to cancel the Friday night service and had invited his congregation to return to Allentown for the last night of the Holy Spirit conference.

There was excitement in the air when Pastor Freidzon came up to the altar to present his message. He urged us to get ready for God to do something extraordinary that evening. He gave a message from 2 Kings 5:10, in which Elisha instructed Naaman, "Go, wash yourself seven times in the Jordan, and your flesh will be restored and you will be cleansed." Just as Naaman was told that he would be healed from leprosy following his seventh dip in the Jordan, Pastor Freidzon told all of us, "Tonight is your seventh dip!" Reminding us that God had instructed the Israelites to go out and claim the land that He had promised (Deuteronomy 1:6–9), Claudio told the congregation, "Go out into the land. . . . You will be a blessing in your office, in the hospital, in your neighborhood!"

He ended with a prayer and invited all who desired to be touched to come forward to receive an anointing from him and other members of the ministry team. He then asked the praise band to sing while people were coming forward. About five minutes into this time of impartation, Pastor Freidzon interrupted the praise band to permit Javier to present a testimony to the entire congregation. Javier took a few tentative steps and then began walking normally for the first time in more than five years! He testified that he had just been healed and didn't have words to describe what had just happened to him.

"It's God! It's God!" Claudio exclaimed in an excited voice. At that moment he took Javier's walker and held it up for all to see as the entire congregation raised a clap offering and gave shouts of praise to the Lord!

That evening everyone present at the Church on the Move witnessed a remarkable visitation from the Lord. All of us knew we had experienced a dramatic encounter with the living God, and we heard many stories of others who were healed of diabetes, chronic digestive problems, and other infirmities.

Javier had broken his back in 1996 when he fell on the ice while working. In that accident he suffered a disc herniation that resulted in degenerative disc disease. After consultations with twenty-nine doctors, surgery, and numerous medical treatments, he was declared permanently disabled. But by his faith and the grace of God, Javier is now strong enough to walk for miles without any kind of assistance, and he can even lift people into the air. He is completely free from the chronic pain and nausea that he suffered prior to the conference, and the calluses that had developed on his hands from constant use of the walker have now disappeared.

Since his healing Javier has spent many hours ministering to hospital patients and others who need spiritual encouragement, and he may frequently be seen skipping joyfully through the streets of Dunellen. He has no explanation of how God healed him, but he is eternally grateful to God and to his many friends who prayed for years for his healing.[3]

That night I could not stop thinking about Jehovah Rapha and His ability to instantly heal conditions that do not respond to any available medical treatments. As I drove from Allentown back to New Jersey, I thanked the Lord for healing Javier's back in such an extraordinary way. Then it became clear to me that Javier's healing had actually started during the conference with Pastor Scataglini the previous fall. Sergio's message, "Preparing the Way for the Lord," had deeply touched Javier and convinced him that he needed to clean up several things in his life. After that first Allentown conference he began reading his Bible more regularly, praying more regularly and more intensely, and he changed several habits that had been hindering his walk with the Lord.

Javier's healing affected me more than the healing of my injured leg at the 1999 conference in Cedar Rapids. While both of these events included extraordinary, instantaneous healings, I realized that in both conferences the work of preparing for the coming of the Lord preceded the spiritual renewal that produced physical healing.

As I drove home along Interstate 78, I began to understand why Isaiah and John the Baptist urged believers to prepare the way for the Lord by repenting and developing habits of holiness. These two conferences in Allentown had affected me so profoundly that I realized the Lord was giving me a new message of hope to share with others. Never again would I drive along Highway 78 without thinking about God's great power and love, and I was being led to share this message with the nations. The Lord was clearly calling me to be an "ambassador for Christ" (see 2 Corinthians 5:20), both in the U.S. and abroad. Interstate 78 had become my personal "Highway of Holiness," where I am called to remind the people that God is still in the business of restoring bodies, cities, and even entire nations.

What I had seen in Allentown on March 9, 2001, was concrete evidence that God fully intends to fulfill all the prophecies of restoration that He gave centuries ago. In

> **Interstate 78 had become my personal "Highway of Holiness," where I am called to remind the people that God is still in the business of restoring bodies, cities, and even entire nations.**

Isaiah 35:4–8, we read that all of creation will be changed by the power of God:

> *[S]ay to those with fearful hearts, "Be strong, do not fear; your God will come, he will come with vengeance; with divine retribution he will come to save you." Then will the eyes of the blind be opened and the ears of the deaf unstopped. **Then will the lame leap like a deer,** and the mute tongue shout for joy. Water will gush forth in the wilderness and streams in the desert. The burning sand will become a pool, the thirsty ground bubbling springs. In the haunts where the jackals once lay, grass and reeds and papyrus will grow. **And a highway will be there; it will be called the Way of Holiness.** The unclean will not journey on it; it*

will be for those who walk in that Way; wicked fools will not go about on it. [emphasis added]

Javier dancing in Washington Square Park, Dunellen, New Jersey, six months after his miraculous healing

PRAYER

O Lord Jesus, create in me an ever-increasing desire to know you. Give me a transformed heart that seeks to learn how wide and long and high and deep is your love for me. Remove all of my sinful ways and consume me with the fire of your holiness. Lead me to proclaim freedom for the captives, the lame, and the oppressed. And as I experience the eyes of the blind being opened, the ears of the deaf being unstopped, and the lame leaping like a deer, show me the Way of Holiness that you have prepared for me to walk. Amen.

PART TWO

Past Awakenings

MARTINS CREEK, PA
CROSSWICKS, NJ

Aflame for God

That which was divinely refreshing and strengthening to my soul was that I saw that God is the same as He was in the days of Elijah. Was enabled to wrestle with God by prayer in a more affectionate, fervent, humble, intense, and importunate manner than I have for many months past. Nothing seemed too hard for God to perform; nothing too great for me to hope for from Him.
　　—David Brainerd, **Life and Diary,** *November 3, 1743*

We come now to the first of four stops on my Highway of Holiness. Our journey begins at Martins Creek, Pennsylvania, which is six miles north of Easton along the Delaware River. Today you can get there by taking the last exit on Interstate 78 in Pennsylvania, but traveling there was much more difficult in colonial times. In 1744 a young Presbyterian missionary named David Brainerd was called to minister to the Delaware Indians at this location, which was then called "Forks of Delaware." The Delaware tribe was reputed to be very ferocious and worshiped pagan gods.

Brainerd lived from 1718 to 1747 and spent his last five years witnessing to the Indians in Massachusetts, Pennsylvania, and New Jersey. He had been an outstanding student at Yale College but was expelled in February 1742 after making inappropriate comments about two faculty members. After the expulsion he went into a

period of deep soul-searching, during which he was greatly comforted by Isaiah's prophetic verses about the suffering of the
Messiah: "Yet it pleased the LORD to bruise him . . . [and] make his
soul an offering for sin" (Isaiah 53:10, KJV). He became aware that
God was calling him to minister to the "savage" American Indians
rather than serve as a pulpit minister at a comfortable Congrega-
tional church in his home state of Connecticut. The April 6, 1742,
entry in his *Life and Diary* contains the following remarks:

> *Found myself willing, if God should so order it, to suffer banish-*
> *ment from my native land, among the heathen, that I might do*
> *something for their salvation, in distresses and deaths of any kind.*
> *Then God gave me to wrestle earnestly for others, for the kingdom*
> *of Christ in the world, and for dear Christian friends. I felt weaned*
> *from the world and from my own reputation amongst men, willing*
> *to be despised and to be a gazing stock for the world to behold. It*
> *is impossible for me to express how I then felt. I had not much joy,*
> *but some sense of the majesty of God, which made me as it were*
> *tremble.*[1]

At the suggestion of Aaron Burr, Sr., and Jonathan Edwards,
Brainerd was ordained as a minister at the First Presbyterian Church
in Newark, New Jersey, in June of 1744 and was commissioned at
that time to be an Indian missionary through the Scottish Society for
the Propagation of Christian Knowledge. His extensive diaries and
journal, which were originally written as mission reports to the
Scottish Society, became world-famous after his death in 1747.
They were published that year by Jonathan Edwards and have been
in print continuously for more than 250 years.

Let's go back in time to the summer of 1744 and join Brainerd
as he prepares to meet the Indians after his exhausting journey from
Newark over what he called the "hideous mountains" of New Jersey
and eastern Pennsylvania.

*Marker at David Brainerd's home site
at Martins Creek, Pennsylvania*

Nothing Is Too Difficult for God

The young missionary sat on the bank of an inlet of the Susque-hanna River, watching a colony of beavers build a dam across the stream. On this beautiful evening David Brainerd had just entered the land of the Delaware Indians. A Bible rested on his lap, turned to his favorite verse, John 7:37: "If any man thirst, let him come unto me, and drink" (KJV).

He was so absorbed in the scene before him, and his burning desire to minister to the First Nations people, that he was unaware that the sharp eyes of a party of Delaware scouts were riveted upon him the entire night. He knelt praying to God for hours, uncon-scious that a rattlesnake crept to his side, lifted up its head as if to strike, flicked out its tongue near his face, and then, without any apparent reason, slithered swiftly back into the wilderness.

The next morning he rode his horse over to the Indians' settlement, expecting a hostile reception from them. But to his surprise, the whole tribe came out to meet him as he approached their wigwams. "The Great Spirit is with the paleface!" said the scouts, and the tribe gave him a hero's welcome that morning.[2]

Brainerd knew that his mission was humanly impossible, but that with God everything was possible. He had studied the lives of Elijah, Moses, Abraham, and Paul and wanted to experience the glory of God just as these patriarchs had. In the words of Eugene Myers Harrison, "Brainerd longed to be *AFLAME FOR GOD,* living, like Moses, a life of self-abasement to His service and glory; . . . being like Elijah, a man fervent and mighty in prayer; . . . his life, like Abraham's, being characterized by the holy piety of one on pilgrimage to eternity; . . . living, like Paul, to preach Christ and to share his sufferings unto the salvation of souls."[3]

> **Brainerd had studied the lives of Elijah, Moses, Abraham, and Paul and wanted to experience the glory of God just as these patriarchs had.**

That first summer of 1744 he commissioned an Indian man, Moses Tinda Tautamy, to be his translator while he preached at Forks of Delaware. Tautamy was about fifty years of age and was well acquainted with the pagan services and customs of his people, but Brainerd reports that "he seemed to have little or no impression of religion on his mind, and in that respect was very unfit for his work, being incapable of understanding and communicating to others many things of importance."[4] Within a month, however, Brainerd reports that Tautamy was "somewhat awakened to a concern for his soul" and began to seek the Lord earnestly for his salvation.[5]

Tautamy's baptism in July 1745 was a turning point in Brainerd's ministry. In a few months the interpreter began to understand the basics of Christian doctrine and could explain Brainerd's sermons to his people quite effectively. As Brainerd summarized his first year of ministry among the Delaware Indians, he was impressed by how God had equipped Tautamy for his job as interpreter:

> *He had likewise, to appearance, an experimental acquaintance with divine things; and it pleased God at this season to inspire his mind with longing desires for the conversion of the Indians, and to give him admirable zeal and fervency in addressing them in order thereto. And it is remarkable, that when I was favored with any special assistance in any work and enabled to speak with more than common freedom, fervency, and power, under a lively and affecting sense of divine things, he was usually affected in the same manner almost instantly, and seemed at once quickened and enabled to speak in the same pathetic language, and under the same influence that I did. A surprising energy often accompanied the Word at such seasons; so that the face of the whole assembly would be apparently changed almost in an instant, and tears and sobs became common among them.[6]*

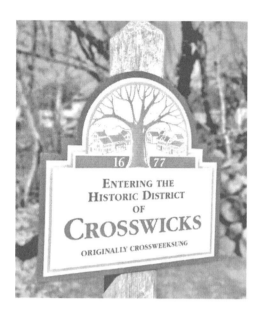

Revival Breaks Out at Crossweeksung

After more than a year of preaching at Forks of Delaware, Brainerd was discouraged by the lack of success he had in winning converts to Jesus Christ. He heard about another settlement of Indians at Crossweeksung, New Jersey,[7] located about ninety miles southeast of Forks of Delaware, and began preaching there in June of 1745. On August 4 of that year, Brainerd began noticing an unusual change in the behavior of the Indians:

> *Now a change in their manners began to appear very visible. In the evening when they came to sup together, they would not taste a morsel till they had sent me to come and ask a blessing on their*

food; at which time sundry of them wept, especially when I minded
them how they had in times past eaten their feasts in honor to dev-
ils, and neglected to thank God for them.[8]

The next day Brainerd preached from his favorite text, John
7:37—which in NIV reads "On the last and greatest day of the
Feast, Jesus stood and said in a loud voice, 'If anyone is thirsty, let
him come to me and drink'"—and the fear of the Lord came upon
the Indians.

In my discourse addressed the Indians in particular, who sat by
themselves in a part of the house; at which time one or two of them
were struck with deep concern, as they afterwards told me, who had
been little affected before; others had their concern increased to a
considerable degree. In the evening (the greater part of them being
at the house where I lodged), I discoursed to them, and found them
universally engaged about their souls' concern, inquiring, "What
they should do to be saved?" And all their conversation among
themselves turned upon religious matters, in which they were much
assisted by my interpreter, who was with them day and night.[9]

On the afternoon of August 5 about forty adult Indians came to
Crossweeksung to attend Brainerd's daily worship service. As he
preached to them from 1 John 4:10, the message of God's love
began to penetrate their hearts in a powerful way:

Then divine truths were attended with a surprising influence, and
produced a great concern among them. There were scarce three in
forty that could refrain from tears and bitter cries. They all, as
one, seemed in an agony of soul to obtain an interest in Christ;
and the more I discoursed of the love and compassion of God in
sending His Son to suffer for the sins of men; and the more I invit-
ed them to come and partake of His love, the more their distress
was aggravated, because they felt themselves unable to come. It

was surprising to see how their hearts seemed to be pierced with the tender and melting invitations of the gospel, when there was not a word of terror spoken to them. . . . Surprising were now the doings of the Lord, that I can say no less of this day (and I need say no more of it) than that the arm of the Lord was powerfully and marvelously revealed in it.[10]

The next day several Indians were awakened as Brainerd preached about Christ's suffering from Isaiah 53:3–10. Brainerd marveled that God seemed to be calling them from remote places to attend his worship services.

On the afternoon of August 8 he preached from Luke 14:16–24, which describes Jesus' parable in which the master who was preparing a great banquet instructed his servants to "Go out to the roads and country lanes and make them come in, so that my house will be full" (v. 23). After he spoke to a audience of about sixty-five persons, he observed that the power of God seemed to descend upon the crowd "like a rushing mighty wind" and bore down upon all with an "astonishing energy."[11] His diary entry for that day states,

I stood amazed at the influence that seized the audience almost universally, and could compare it to nothing more aptly than the irresistible force of a mighty torrent, or swelling deluge, that with its insupportable weight and pressure bears down and sweeps before it whatever is in its way. Almost all persons of all ages were bowed down with concern together, and scarce one was able to withstand the shock of this surprising operation. . . .

They were almost universally praying and crying for mercy, in every part of the house, and many out of doors, and numbers could neither go nor stand. Their concern was so great, each one for himself, that none seemed to take any notice of those about them, but each prayed freely for himself. And, I am to think, they were to their own apprehension as much retired as if they had been, indi-

vidually, by themselves in the thickest desert; or, I believe rather, that they thought nothing about any but themselves, and their own states, and so were everyone praying apart, although all together.

It seemed to me there was now an exact fulfillment of that prophecy, Zechariah 12:10–12; for there was now "a great mourning," like the mourning of Hadadrimmon, and each seemed to "mourn apart." Methought this had a near resemblance to the day of God's power, mentioned in Joshua 10:14. I must say I never saw any day like it in all respects. It was a day wherein I am persuaded the Lord did much to destroy the kingdom of darkness among this people today. . . . All were afraid of the anger of God and of everlasting misery as the desert of their sins. [12]

On August 10 he preached to the Indians from Luke 19:10: "For the Son of man is come to seek and to save that which was lost" (KJV). He writes,

I had not discoursed long before their concern rose to a great degree, and the house was filled with cries and groans. When I insisted on the compassion and care of the Lord Jesus Christ for those that were lost, who thought themselves undone and could find no way of escape, this melted them down the more and aggravated their distress that they could not find and come to so kind a Saviour.

Surely persons, who before had been but slightly awakened, were now deeply wounded with a sense of their own sin and misery. One man in particular, who was never before awakened, was now made to feel that "the word of my Lord was quick and powerful, sharper than any two-edged sword." He seemed to be pierced at heart with distress, and his concern appeared most rational and scriptural; for he said that all the wickedness of his past life was brought fresh to his remembrance, and he saw all the vile actions he had done formerly as if done but yesterday.[13]

The size of the assembly began to increase day by day, and Brainerd was amazed that God was now orchestrating a powerful revival at Crossweeksung:

God is powerfully at work among them! True and genuine convictions of sin are daily promoted in many instances, and some are newly awakened from time to time, although some few, who felt a commotion in their passions in days past, seem now to discover that their hearts were never duly affected. . . . I never saw the work of God appear so independent of means as at this time. I discoursed to the people, and spent what, I suppose, had a proper tendency to promote convictions. But God's manner of working upon them appeared so entirely supernatural and above means that I could scarce believe He used me as an instrument, or what I spake as means of carrying on His work. It seemed, I thought, to have no connection with, nor dependence upon means in any respect. Although I could not but continue to use the means which I thought proper for the promotion of the work, yet God seemed, as I apprehended, to work entirely without them. I seemed to do nothing, and indeed to have nothing to do, but to "stand still and see the salvation of God." I found myself obliged and delighted to say, "Not unto us," not unto instruments and means, "but to thy name be glory." God appeared to work entirely alone, and I saw no room to attribute any part of this work to any created arm.[14]

The Entire Village is Transformed

As the revival progressed Brainerd noted not only that the Indians were coming to a saving faith in Jesus Christ, but also that their lives and their economy were being transformed:

The effects of this work have likewise been very remarkable.

I doubt not that many of these people have gained more doctrinal knowledge of divine truths, since I first visited them in June
last, than could have been instilled into their minds by the most
diligent use of proper and instructive means for whole years together, without such a divine influence. Their pagan notions and idol-
atrous practices seem to be entirely abandoned in these parts. They
are regulated and appear regularly disposed in the affairs of marriage. They seem generally divorced from drunkenness, their dar-
ling vice, and the "sin that easily besets them"; so that I do not
know of more than two or three who have been my steady hearers,
that have drunk to excess since I first visited them, although before
it was common for some or other of them to be drunk almost every
day. Some of them seem now to fear this sin in particular more
than death itself.

A principle of honesty and justice appears in many of them,
and they seem concerned to discharge their old debts, which they
have neglected, and perhaps, scarce thought of for years past.
Their manner of living is much more decent and comfortable than
formerly, having now the benefits of that money which they used to
consume upon strong drink. Love seems to reign among them, especially those who have given evidences of having passed a saving
change. I never saw any appearance of bitterness or censoriousness
in these, nor any disposition to "esteem themselves better than others," who had not received the like mercy.[15]

Although Brainerd insisted on several months of probation before he would baptize them, by the following March more than 130
Indians had come to a saving faith in Jesus at the Crossweeksung
revival. The revival spread to Forks of Delaware and produced a
permanent impact on the spiritual state of First Nations people. A
century later missionaries to Indian tribes living in Wisconsin met

some descendants of David Brainerd's "people" from Crossweek-sung. One very old woman described how her grandmother had spoken about him:

> He was a young man; he was a lovely man; he was a staff to walk with; he went from house to house to talk religion; that was his way.[16]

Although he died of tuberculosis before reaching the age of thirty, his life and work among the Indians have inspired countless men and women to enter the mission field, including William Carey and Henry Martyn. It was no wonder that George Whitefield often mentioned David Brainerd as he preached to crowds in fields and marketplaces throughout the Thirteen Colonies.

How Brainerd Operated in the Spirit

People who heard David Brainerd preach knew that he was "aflame for God." His passionate preaching; his daily prayer burdens for the Indians; his commitment to evangelistic, Calvinistic preaching; and his unwavering commitment to "wear out my life in God's service and glory" were major marks of his ministry to the Indians. An observer who looked analytically at his work might declare that he was a "one-man revival."

But Brainerd would certainly not agree with this assessment. He understood well that his calling was to preach the gospel as faithfully as he could. Whether his preaching was to a handful of Indians (as it was at the beginning of his ministry) or to three thousand men and women of European descent (at William Tennent's Neshaminy church in present-day Warminster, Pennsylvania), Brainerd knew that the battle for souls was the Lord's. His diary entry for June 27, 1744, reads as follows:

*My great concern was for the conversion of the heathen to God;
and the Lord helped me to plead with Him for it. Towards noon,
rode up to the Indians in order to preach to them. While going, my
heart went up to God in prayer for them; could freely tell God He
knew that the cause was not mine which I was engaged in; but it
was His own cause and it would be for His own glory to convert
the poor Indians. Blessed be God, I felt no desire of their conversion
that I might receive honor from the world, as being the instrument
of it.*[17]

In his student days at Yale College he had learned that both the
Puritans and the "New Light" revivalists (including George Whitefield and Gilbert Tennent) believed that spiritual regeneration (or
"rebirth") occurs in stages. These New Light leaders believed that
the first act in regeneration brought a conviction of guilt and
misery. After this initial step, it was felt that the preacher should
employ the "Terrors of the Law" to cause the hearers to fear for the
condition of their souls without Christ. When these two steps were
done, the New Light revivalists believed that the person was ready
to receive God.[18]

But Brainerd and his theological mentor, Jonathan Edwards, did
not believe that God always followed this model of regeneration. In
his ***Life and Diary,*** for example, Brainerd tells us,

*When persons have been awakened to a solemn concern for their
souls by hearing the more awful truths of God's Word and the terrors of the divine law insisted upon, it has usually in such cases
been objected by some that such persons were only frighted with a
fearful noise of hell and damnation; and that there was no evidence that their concern was the effect of a divine influence. But
God has left no room for this objection in the present case, **this
work of grace having been begun and carried on by***

> *almost one continued strain of gospel invitation to per-*
> *ishing sinners.*[19] [emphasis original]

Although Brainerd did not preach a message of "fire and brim-
stone" like many Puritans and evangelists of his day, it is nevertheless clear that Brainerd's Indian revivals were characterized by
Knowledge and Fear of the Lord. While his message was a "pure
gospel invitation" that did not shame or threaten his listeners with
the "Terrors of the Law," even a cursory review of Brainerd's
writings reveals that he constantly lived in awe and reverence for
Almighty God. On July 6, 1744, for example, he journaled the
following remarks:

> *Awoke this morning in the fear of God. Soon called to mind my*
> *sadness in the evening past and spent my first waking minutes in*
> *prayer for sanctification, that my soul may be washed from its*
> *exceeding pollution and defilement. . . . But blessed be God, I have*
> *less desire to live for any of the pleasures of the world, than ever I*
> *had. I long and love to be a pilgrim. And want grace to imitate*
> *the life, labors and sufferings of Paul among the heathen.*[20]

As Brainerd noted, once he began preaching the gospel, he
could tell whether he was preaching with "freedom" and "favor"
from God. When these conditions were present, God would
supernaturally melt hearts while he preached the Word. From his
journal entry for December 15, 1745, for example, we learn how
this happened at Crossweeksung:

> *Preached to the Indians from Luke 13:24–28. Divine truths fell*
> *with weight and power upon the audience, and seemed to reach the*
> *hearts of many. . . . This was an amazing season of grace! "The*
> *word of the Lord," this day, "was quick and powerful, sharper than*
> *a two-edged sword," and pierced the hearts of many. The assembly*
> *was greatly affected, and deeply wrought upon; yet without so*

much apparent commotion of the passions, as was usual in the beginning of this work of grace. The impressions made by the Word of God upon the audience appeared solid, rational, and deep, worthy of the solemn truths by means of which they were produced, and far from being the effects of any sudden fright, or groundless perturbation of mind.

Oh, how did the hearers seem to bow under the weight of divine truths! And how evident did it now appear that they received and felt them, "not as the word of man, but as the word of God!" None can frame a just idea of the appearance of our assembly at this time, but those who have seen a congregation solemnly awed and deeply impressed by the special power and influence of divine truths delivered to them in the name of God.[21]

From Brainerd's writings it appears that he was able to sense whether God was anointing his message so that the weight of the gospel teachings had impacted his listeners. When this anointing was present, Brainerd noted both that he had "unusual freedom" and that his interpreter "addressed the Indians with admirable fervency, and scarce knew when to leave off."[22] This supernatural efficiency in applying the Word of God to our lives is what we refer to as the "Spirit of Knowledge."[23]

In addition to the Spirit of Knowledge, at least two other spiritual operations appear to have been in effect in these Indian revivals. First, Brainerd notes in the Summary to Part I of his journal,

It is remarkable how God providentially, and in a manner almost unaccountable, called these Indians together to be instructed in the great things that concerned their souls; how He seized their minds with the most solemn and weighty concern for their eternal salvation, as fast as they came to the place where His Word was preached.

> *When I first came into these parts in June, I found not one man at the place I visited, but only four women and a few children. But before I had been there many days, they gathered from all quarters, some from more than twenty miles distant. When I made a second visit in the beginning of August, some came more than forty miles to hear me.*
>
> *Many came without any intelligence of what was going on here, and consequently without any design of theirs, so much as to gratify their curiosity. So that it seemed as if God had summoned them together from all quarters for nothing else but to deliver His message to them; and that He did this, with regard to some of them, without making use of any human means, although there were pains taken by some of them to give notice to others at remote places.*[24]

It appears that the Spirit of the Lord[25] was doing a supernatural work to bring men and women to Brainerd's services, with none of the publicity or fanfare that revivalists were using elsewhere during the First Great Awakening. Week after week, an increasing number of Indians traveled long distances to hear Brainerd speak. They crowded around his house at night, crying out in their native language, "Guttummaukalummeh wechaumeh kmeleb Ndah," which in English is translated, "Have mercy on me, and help me to give You my heart."[26]

It is significant to note that all these spiritual operations intensified after the power of God descended "like a mighty rushing wind" on August 8, 1744.[27] This expression is consistent with the description of the "violent wind" that descended on the early church at the Day of Pentecost (Acts 2:2). Other unusual spiritual operations occurred after August 8, including a remarkable conversion of an Indian conjurer who spontaneously came forward and gave up his rattles[28] and an elderly woman who came to the Lord after having a vision in which she saw herself walking up a wide path leading to destruction rather than "striving to enter in at the strait gate" that leads to heaven.[29]

Brainerd was well aware of the controversies that had arisen elsewhere about excessive "enthusiasm" that had occurred in some places during the First Great Awakening, and he also knew that Satan often uses "trances and imaginary views of things"[30] to disrupt genuine works of God. In this case, however, he believed that this particular woman may well have been converted to Jesus Christ as the result of her vision. On this matter he concludes,

> *How far God may make use of the imagination in awakening some persons under these, and such like circumstances, I cannot pretend to determine. Or whether this exercise be from a divine influence, I shall leave others to judge. But this I must say, that its effects hitherto bespeak it to be such. Nor can it, as I see, be accounted for, in a rational way, but from the influence of some spirit, either good or evil. For the woman I am sure, never heard divine things treated of in the manner she now viewed them in; and it would seem strange she should get such a rational notion of them from the mere working of her own fancy, without some superior, or at least foreign aid. Yet I must say, I have looked upon it as one of the glories of this work of grace among the Indians, and a special evidence of its being from a divine influence, that there has, till now, been no appearance of such things, no visionary notions, trances, and imaginations intermixed with those rational convictions of sin, and solid consolations, that numbers have been made the subjects of. And might I have had my desire, there had been no appearance of anything of this nature at all.*[31]

In summary, the major spiritual operations at work in the Brainerd Indian revivals included: (1) the Spirit of the Lord acting to draw people to Brainerd's services and to convict them of their sins, (2) the Spirit of Knowledge applying the Word of God to the life experiences of those who heard the message, and (3) the Fear of the Lord causing them to come to Brainerd asking, "What must I do to be saved?" In addition to these spiritual operations, the stories about the conversion of the conjurer and the elderly woman with the vision suggest that the Spirit of Power and the Spirit of Counsel, respectively, may also have been in operation in these special circumstances. We will return to this topic in Chapter Nine.

PRAYER

Father, cause me to be aflame for Christ like David Brainerd was. Fill me with such a passion for the lost that I begin to weep for each lost soul I meet. And Father, if anyone should come to me in thirst, allow me to quench that thirst with the water of everlasting life. Increase my faith so that I might have single-minded devotion to the advancement of your Kingdom on earth. Remind me that these are the days of Elijah— no less so than in ages past—and that you desire to use my faith, my passion, and my longsuffering to restore all that was lost in the Garden of Eden. Amen.

CHAPTER FIVE

The Day Whitefield Came
to Basking Ridge

When I came to Baskinridge [sic], I found Mr. Davenport had been preaching to the congregation, according to appointment. It consisted of about three thousand people. I had not discoursed long, when, in every part of the congregation, some one or another began to cry out, and almost all were melted into tears. . . . After sermon, Mr. Cross gave notice of an evening lecture in his barn, two miles off. Thither we went, and a great multitude followed. Mr. Gilbert Tennent preached first; and I then began to pray, and gave an exhortation. In about six minutes, one cried out, "He is come, He is come!", and could scarce contain the manifestation of Jesus to his soul. The eager crying of others, for the like favour, obliged me to stop; and I prayed over them, as I saw their agonies and distress increase. . . . Most of the people spent the remainder of the night in prayer and praises. It was a night much to be remembered.
—**George Whitefield's Journals,** *November 5, 1740*

The second stop on my Highway of Holiness is Basking Ridge, New Jersey, which is located on Interstate 78, thirty-six miles east of the Delaware River. In George Whitefield's first trip to New

Jersey in 1739, he became friends with Rev. John Cross, who was the first pastor at the Basking Ridge Presbyterian Church. When Whitefield returned to New Jersey the following year, Rev. Cross invited him to speak outdoors under a magnificent oak tree. Today this tree is more than six hundred years old and is fondly referred to as the "Whitefield Tree" by local residents. Let's go to Basking Ridge and witness the excitement that came during America's first national revival—the "First Great Awakening."

Basking Ridge in the First Great Awakening

George Whitefield's reputation spread through the Thirteen Colonies before he ever stepped foot in New England. His meteoric rise in popularity in England was closely chronicled by Benjamin Franklin and other American newsmen. When the twenty-four-year-old Whitefield announced his plans to travel to America in 1739, he was already the most popular figure in the English-speaking world.[1] Franklin's **Pennsylvania Gazette** and other newspapers announced his departure from England and eagerly awaited his landing in Lewes, Delaware, in the fall of 1739. Frank Lambert describes Whitefield's landing in America in the following words:

> *George Whitefield's arrival in October 1739 changed the scope and character of colonial evangelical revivals. The itinerant, whose English successes had inspired American evangelicals, connected the local awakenings, fashioning them into an intercolonial movement—crafting a national event before the existence of a nation. He proclaimed the message of the new birth in every colony through the spoken and printed word. And he lifted the revivals out of narrow denominational constraints by helping to create a "religious public sphere," in which supporters and opponents of revivalism debated the Great Awakening before a literate, rational,*

and independent audience. *Whitefield's transformation of revivals into a national, public event took place largely outside churches and meetinghouses. Continuing the practice developed in England, he preached in marketplaces and employed newspapers to reach a mass audience.*[2]

One of his first stops in the Colonies was New Brunswick, New Jersey. Whitefield describes his first visit to this revival center in the November 20, 1739, entry of his **Journals:**

Reached here about six last night; and preached to-day, at noon, for near two hours, in worthy Mr. [Gilbert] Tennent's meeting-house, to a large assembly gathered together from all parts; and amongst them, Mr. Tennent told me, was a great number of solid Christians. About three in the afternoon, I preached again; and, at seven, I baptized two children, and preached a third time. Among others who came to hear the Word, were several ministers, whom the Lord has been pleased to honour, in making them instruments of bringing many sons to glory. One was Dutch Calvinistic minister, named Freling Housen [Rev. Theodorus Frelinghuysen], pastor of a congregation about four miles from New Brunswick. He is a worthy old soldier of Jesus Christ, and was the beginner of a great work which I trust the Lord is carrying on in these parts. He has been strongly opposed by his carnal brethren, but God has appeared for him, in a surprising manner, and made him more than conqueror, through His love. He has long since learned to fear him only, who can destroy both body and soul in hell.

Another was Mr. Cross, minister of a congregation of Barking Bridge [sic], about twenty miles from Brunswick. He himself told me of many wonderful and sudden conversions that had been wrought by the Lord under his ministry. For some time, eight or nine used to come to him together, in deep distress of soul; and, I think, he said, three hundred of his congregation, which is not a large one, were brought home to Christ. They are now looked upon as enthusiasts and madmen, and treated as such by those who know not God, and are ignorant of the hidden life of Jesus Christ in their hearts. He is one, who, I believe, would rejoice to suffer for the Lord Jesus. Oh, that I may be likeminded!

On that occasion Whitefield agreed to speak to Mr. Cross's congregation in Basking Ridge the following year. Accordingly, Cross and his associates began making arrangements for White-field's historic Basking Ridge visit twelve months later.

On November 5, 1740, the twenty-five-year-old Whitefield stood beneath the ancient oak tree in Rev. Cross's churchyard and addressed the crowd of three thousand. After an opening address by Rev. James Davenport, Whitefield began his discourse. Almost immediately the crowd "melted into tears." Whitefield records what happened at that point:

A little boy, about eight years of age, wept as though his heart would break. Mr. Cross took him up into the wagon, which so af-fected me, that I broke from my discourse, and told the people that, since old professors were not concerned, God, out of an infant's mouth, was perfecting praise; and the little boy should preach to them. As I was going away, I asked the little boy what he cried for? He answered, his sins. I then asked what he wanted? He answered, Christ.[3]

The crowd that day was several times the population of Basking Ridge, since Whitefield's campaigns customarily were announced for weeks in advance over a large geographic area. Farmers and businessmen came from every town in the area, and all were impacted by the Basking Ridge meeting that November day. In addition to those who joined the Basking Ridge Presbyterian Church, two other congregations were birthed through Whitefield's 1740 visit. Farmers from the nearby community of Lamington lived too far away to attend weekly services in Basking Ridge, so they formed their own Presbyterian church immediately after Whitefield's visit. In addition, several people from Basking Ridge became interested in Whitefield's Methodist teachings and began meeting together that fall. Several years later this core group founded St. James Methodist Church. The Basking Ridge Presbyterian Church, the Lamington Presbyterian Church, and St. James Methodist are still active churches today—living wells of revival from the First Great Awakening.

George Whitefield reportedly stood under this ancient oak
tree as he preached to a crowd of three thousand in 1740.
More than six hundred years old, it is still referred to as the
"Whitefield Tree."

Basking Ridge's Legacy Since the First Great Awakening

Basking Ridge played a prominent role during the Revolutionary War. The Continental Army was stationed in nearby Jockey Hollow during the winters of 1779–81, during which time General

Washington frequently visited Basking Ridge. He established a military hospital behind the Presbyterian church and was personally acquainted with the Rev. Samuel Kennedy, who served as pastor from 1751 to 1787. A 1961 history of the Basking Ridge Presbyterian Church states,

> *The latter years of his [Rev. Kennedy's] ministry were a time of agitation and tumult in Basking Ridge, as in all the states and nation, for this was the period of the American Revolution. In 1775 a company of colonial soldiers drilled at the parsonage and at the church. Many members of the congregation went away to fight—35 of them to be laid to their final rest in the old churchyard at Basking Ridge.*
>
> *Tradition has it that General George Washington and his soldiers often rested under the old oak in the cemetery when they rode from their headquarters in Morristown to Pluckemin, where some of the Colonial artillery were stationed. During one of his visits he established a smallpox hospital in Basking Ridge. With another hospital in Jockey Hollow where the main army was encamped, the tribulations of our soldiers were ever before our congregation, and they were constantly being stirred by the sound of drums and marching feet as the men passed through the village.*[4]

The British Army also recognized the strategic significance of Basking Ridge. Washington Irving's classic book, **George Washington: A Biography,** devotes an entire chapter to the British capture of General Charles Lee at Widow White's tavern in December of 1776. Lee was third in command in the Continental Army and was Washington's most experienced general, having been trained in England as a professional soldier. The British news media confidently predicted that the capture of General Lee in Basking Ridge would soon lead to the collapse of the Continental Army.[5]

Basking Ridge has continued to lead and inspire generations of Americans since colonial days. In 1795 the Rev. Robert Finley was installed as pastor at the Basking Ridge Presbyterian Church and as head of its outstanding classical school. His intense style of preaching and teaching impacted Christians throughout central New Jersey. Many prominent pastors, educators, military and government leaders graduated from the Basking Ridge Classical School, and Rev. Finley led his congregation through revivals in 1804 and 1815. During his tenure a Friday night lecture and prayer meeting was instituted, a tradition which continued for at least seventy-five years.[6] Rev. Finley was a strong proponent of freeing Negro slaves and conferred with President James Madison, Henry Clay, Abraham Lincoln, and other prominent national leaders on this matter. He was the prime organizer of the American Colonization Society, which worked toward the establishment of the nation of Liberia.[7]

During the 20th century Basking Ridge became known as a center of corporate power and prestige. When Interstate 287 was constructed in New Jersey in the 1960s, AT&T built suburban complexes at Basking Ridge and several other communities throughout the area. At the time of AT&T's divestiture in 1984, it had more than a million employees and was the largest corporation in the world. When AT&T's fortunes began to decline in the 1990s, its officers realized that the corporation could no longer afford its expensive headquarters in Manhattan, and so they relocated the headquarters to Basking Ridge. Up to the end of the 20th century, visitors to AT&T's corporate headquarters were always struck by the image of Golden Boy, a giant golden statue that symbolized AT&T's illustrious history as the world's leading telecommunications firm. Several other large corporations also recognized that Basking Ridge was an ideal location for corporate office buildings.

Whitefield's Message and Impacts

The similarities and differences between George Whitefield and David Brainerd are striking. Both were brilliant itinerant preachers who were in their early twenties at the beginning of the First Great Awakening. Both preached a Calvinistic message emphasizing the need to be spiritually reborn, and they generally spoke in open-air settings. Both men made numerous trips across New England and the Mid-Atlantic Colonies.

But here the similarities end. Whitefield was born to a middle-class English family in Gloucester in 1714 and excelled in dramatics before receiving a scholarship to attend Pembroke College, Oxford, in 1732. There he quickly befriended John and Charles Wesley and became an avid member of their Holy Club. Under the strict "Methodist" discipline of the Wesleys, he realized that although he believed in Jesus Christ and did good works, he lacked "the new birth" experience that was a necessary condition for receiving salvation. In spiritual despair he withdrew from the Holy Club during Lent in 1735 and committed himself to a six-week fast of all foods except bread and tea. During that time God revealed Himself to Whitefield in a way he never forgot:

> God was pleased to remove the heavy load, to enable me to lay hold of his dear Son by a living faith, and by giving me the Spirit of adoption to seal me, even to the day of everlasting redemption.
>
> O! with what joy—joy unspeakable—even joy that was full of and big with glory, was my soul filled when the weight of sin went off, and an abiding sense of the love of God broke in upon my disconsolate soul! Surely it was a day to be had in everlasting re-membrance. My joys were like a springtide and overflowed the banks.[8]

Unlike Brainerd, who was moody and tended toward depression, Whitefield was an optimist and a uniquely gifted orator who addressed crowds of up to 50,000 people—without the benefit of modern electronic sound equipment. He undoubtedly spoke to the largest audiences ever congregated to hear religious messages prior to the invention of electronic speakers and amplifiers. Gary Kellner describes Whitefield's gift of evangelism as follows:

> *Few evangelists ever touched the masses like George Whitefield. Benjamin Franklin recalled his unparalleled impact on Philadelphia: "It was wonderful to see the Change soon made in the Manners of our Inhabitants. It seem'd as if all the World were growing Religious; so that One could not walk through the Town [Philadelphia] in an Evening without Hearing Psalms sung in different Families on every Street."*
>
> *Whether leading citizens like Benjamin Franklin, coal miners in England, or townspeople in the colonies, George Whitefield moved them all. Unquestionably, he was the greatest evangelist of his time.*[9]

Following the English tradition of Howell Harris, Whitefield became a master of marketplace preaching. His oratorical and dramatics gifts were ideally suited for preaching to crowds of all classes, and his spirited, persuasive style of preaching stood in stark contrast to the formal pulpit preaching of the Anglican pastors of his day. While his sermons were based on solid, Calvinist theology, his presentations became dramatic events. He repeatedly visited all the Colonies, and it was estimated that fully one-third of all Americans heard him speak during the three decades in which he preached in this country.

Lambert summarizes Whitefield's impact on America by contrasting his style with that of Jonathan Edwards:

> *Whitefield introduced a new model of revivalism to America, a paradigm which contrasted with that employed by Edwards. Ed-*

wards embraced a communal approach in which a community's pastor led the entire village or town in a spiritual awakening. Conversion led to reform in this local perspective. Specifically, Northampton's revival resulted in an observable change of behavior among the town's youth. Before the revival, young people had, according to Edwards, roamed the lanes and roads in loud boisterous gangs; afterwards they began to convene for prayer and exhortation. Whitefield, on the other hand, lifted his gaze beyond a community and preached to all who would listen. He delivered his message to a mass audience consisting of disconnected individuals throughout the colonies. In the words of one historian, Whitefield set out "to transform the entire nation."[10]

How the Revival Ended

Whitefield's 1739–40 campaign left an indelible mark on the American Colonies. By the time he returned to England in late 1740, however, he had created controversies from South Carolina to Massachusetts. Mark Noll's insightful book, ***The Rise of Evangelicalism: The Age of Edwards, Whitefield, and the Wesleys,*** summarizes Whitefield's mixed legacy as follows:

Whitefield's influence in America—because of this tour but also his six other visits and the flood of writing by and about him— was momentous. He helped confirm American Presbyterians in a much more consistently evangelical course than their fellow Presbyterians in Scotland and Ireland were pursuing. Similarly, he contributed a strong evangelical note to New England Congregationalism and so hastened the growth of parties (traditional vs. evangelical vs. liberal) that soon splintered this once strong establishment. He inspired many who would later become leaders of Baptist and Methodist churches. He was also a personal bridge that connected many previously isolated groups, including some

Quakers and German immigrant congregations, with the Dissenting denominations that were his main supporters.

In all his activities Whitefield combined an extraordinary disregard for inherited church traditions with a breathtaking entrepreneurial spirit. The willingness to innovate made him immensely popular to the colonies and also promoted among later American evangelicals a similar disregard for Christian traditions. Yet his large, quick actions and urge to create left an ambiguous legacy, since it was much easier for Whitefield to announce grand plans than to carry them through. . . .

Whitefield was both winsomely naïve and casually judgmental in ways that continue to mark at least some strands of evangelicalism in America. As an example, he appears to have formed his unfavorable judgment on Harvard College—"Discipline is at a low ebb. Bad books are become fashionable among the tutors and students"—after less than a day in Cambridge, Massa-

> **The three leaders who preached in Basking Ridge all made serious errors of judgment that ultimately quenched the work of the Holy Spirit during the First Great Awakening.**

chusetts. Similarly, his frequently harsh words about unconverted ministers probably spoke to a genuine problem, but the supreme self-assurance that characterized those words and the paucity of hard evidence on which they rested amounted to irresponsibility. . . .

Much of what Whitefield did was admirable by any standard, and his commitment to Christ-centered preaching was a shining beacon. But while his character and purpose possessed great integrity, there was no consistency to his broader actions, no depth to *his thinking about culture. Ready, fire, aim was his style. In a word, much that would be best and much that would be worst in the later history of evangelicals in America was anticipated by Whitefield in this one stirring year.*[11]

The three men who preached in Basking Ridge—Whitefield, Gilbert Tennent, and James Davenport—were mightily used of God to bring hundreds of thousands of men and women to Christ in the Thirteen Colonies. In fact, scholars who have studied 18th century church records have estimated that fully ten percent of the population of New England joined the church during the First Great Awakening, and similar church growth occurred in the other American Colonies.[12]

At the same time, however, all three of these leaders made serious errors of judgment that ultimately quenched the work of the Holy Spirit during the First Great Awakening. Whitefield, in particular, was so focused on the new birth that he denounced clergy who had not had "an immediate experience of the Spirit that assured them of their faith."[13] Jonathan Edwards had concerns about Whitefield's errors of judgment and urged him to soften his criticisms of pastors who opposed revival, but there is no record of Whitefield's response to Edwards in this regard. The following comments from the 19th century editor of Edwards' *Memoirs* are revealing:

This indiscreet advice had, at times, too much influence, and occasioned in some places sundering of churches and congregations, in others the removal of ministers, and in others the separation of individuals from the communion of their brethren. It thus introduced contentions and quarrels into churches and families, alienated ministers from each other, and from their people, and produced, in the places where these consequences were most discernible, a wide-spread and riveted prejudice against revivals of religion. It is deserving perhaps of inquiry, Whether the subsequent slumber of the American church, for nearly seventy years, may not be ascribed, in an important degree, to the fatal re-action of these unhappy measures.

There can be no doubt that on Mr. Whitefield (although by his multiplied and successful labours he was the means of incalculable good to the churches of America, as well as to those of England and Scotland) these evils are, to a considerable degree, to be charged, as having first led the way in this career of irregularity and disorder. He did not go as far as some of his followers; but he opened a wide door, and went great lengths, in these forbidden paths; and his imitators, having less discretion and experience, ventured, under the cover of his example, even beyond the limits which he himself was afraid to pass. His published journals show, that he was accustomed to decide too authoritatively, whether others, particularly ministers, were converted; as well as to insist that churches ought to remove those, whom they regarded as unconverted ministers; and that individual Christians or minorities of churches, where a majority refused to do this, were bound to separate themselves. Mr. Edwards, wholly disapproving of this conduct, conversed with Mr. Whitefield freely, in the presence of others, about his practice of pronouncing ministers, and other members of the Christian church, unconverted; and declares that he supposed him to be of the opinion, that unconverted ministers ought not to be continued in the ministry; and that he supposed that he endeavoured to propagate this opinion, and a practice agreeable thereto. The same may be said, in substance, of Mr. G[ilbert]. Tennent, Mr. [Samuel] Finley, and Mr. [James] Davenport, all of whom became early convinced of their error, and with Christian sincerity openly acknowledged it.[14]

How Whitefield Operated in the Spirit

Like most of the prominent revivalists in the First Great Awakening, Whitefield was filled with the Spirit of the Lord and operated in Knowledge and Fear of the Lord. Noll summarizes quite well how these two spiritual operations were in effect in Whitefield's open-air preaching:

> *Characteristically, Whitefield would announce and read a text of Scripture, pray audibly and sometimes also silently (often on his knees), and then begin his discourse. A Boston listener described what happened next on one occasion: "To have seen him when he first commenced, one would have thought him anything but enthusiastic and glowing; but, as he proceeded, his heart warmed with his subject, and his manner became impetuous, till, forgetful of everything around him, he seemed to kneel at the throne of Jehovah and to beseech in agony for his fellow-beings." The same observer described Whitefield's verbal agility in once using a passing thunderstorm to compare human life to a transitory cloud, the wrath of God to a lightning bolt, and his divine mercy to the sun emerging after rain. When asked for a text of this particular sermon for the printer, Whitefield replied, "I have no objection, if you will print the lightning, thunder, and rainbow with it."*[15]

Rev. William McCullough makes a similar point in describing how fear and agony combined in Whitefield's preaching in Cambalusing, Scotland:

> *I have reason to believe that upwards of five hundred souls have been awakened, brought under a deep conviction of sin, and a feeling sense of their lost condition. Most of these have, I trust, been savingly brought home to God. I do not include in this number such as have been found to be mere pretenders, nor such as have had nothing in their exercise beyond a dread of hell.*[16]

Most preachers in the colonial period—or today, for that matter—would be regarded as unusually anointed if they operated in these three spiritual areas. But what made Whitefield's preaching most extraordinary, in my opinion, was that he also operated in Counsel and Power. A casual examination of his ***Journals*** provides dozens of illustrations of these latter two spiritual operations. For example, we read how Counsel and Power worked together in his campaign in Philadelphia on November 9, 1739:

> *Read prayers and preached as usual in the morning; and perceived the congregation still increased. Visited a sick person, for whom I was sent for, and felt the power of the Lord was also present, both with him and those who attended him. Most wept at the preaching of faith. I was visited in a kind manner by the minister of the parish; and preached again at six in the evening, from the Court House steps. I believe there were nearly two thousand more present to-night than last night. Even in London, I never perceived so profound a silence. Before I came, all was hushed exceedingly quiet. The night was clear, but not cold. Lights were in most of the windows all around us for a considerable distance. The people did not seem weary of standing, nor was I weary of speaking. The Lord endued me with power from on high. My heart was enlarged and warmed with Divine love. My soul was so carried out in prayer, that I thought I could have continued my discourse all night. After I came home, some desired to join me in family prayer; and in that exercise the Divine Presence was manifest amongst us. Surely God is favourable unto this people. At present they seem most gladly to receive the Word. Lord, I beseech Thee, shew forth Thy glory more and more; and grant that much people in this place may be enabled to believe on Thee.*[17]

Wherever Whitefield went, the crowds were captivated by his spiritual authority (which is related to the Spirit of Counsel) and by the extraordinary power of his voice. Whitefield frequently noted that the strength of his voice was in fact greater the more spiritual opposition he felt in the crowd.[18] But then there were also many extraordinary happenings in many of his rallies—people falling down, amazing healings, and the like. In Bexley, England, for example, a group of Anglican bishops criticized his style of open-air preaching and demanded signs of his authority. Whitefield summed up this incident in his *Journals* as follows:

> **They say it is not regular, our going out into the high-ways and hedges, and compelling poor sinners to come in.** *We ought not so to beseech them to be reconciled to God. They desire to know by what authority we preach, and ask, "What sign shewest thou that thou dost these things?" But, alas! what further sign would they require? We went not into the fields till we were excluded from the churches; and has not God set His seal to our ministry in an extraordinary manner? Have not many that were spiritually blind received their sight? Many that have been lame strengthened to run the way of God's commandments? Have not the deaf heard? The lepers been cleansed? The dead raised? And the poor had the Gospel preached unto them? That these notable miracles have been wrought, not in our own names, or by our own power, but in the Name and by the power of Jesus of Nazareth cannot be denied. And yet they require a sign.*[19] [emphasis added]

Thus, we see that Whitefield's life and ministry demonstrated all but two of the seven spiritual operations described in Isaiah 11:2 (and noted in Chapter Two)—the Spirit of the Lord, Counsel, Power, Knowledge, and Fear of the Lord. **But none of the source documents I reviewed indicated that he operated in Wisdom or Understanding!** And this observation helps to explain why his legacy is so mixed: His weaknesses in judgment and in dealing with his critics were exactly parallel to his lifelong deficiencies in

Wisdom and spiritual Understanding. What a tragedy it is that this extraordinarily gifted man of God is remembered by many as a "pedlar in divinity" or as a "divine dramatist" rather than as a tireless evangelist who brought countless thousands of men and women to Jesus Christ and gave the Colonies a desire for American independence.

To the men who served in the Continental Army George Whitefield was a spiritual giant. As Stephen Mansfield states in his recent biography of Whitefield, this English evangelist was

> . . . [t]heir spiritual father, the man who called them back to Christ and to Christ's purpose for their land. It was his vision of freedom for both soul and society that they now fought to defend. . . . [T]he fires of revival spread into a blaze of freedom—and forged a nation in the process.[20]

The thirty-five Revolutionary War soldiers buried in the Basking Ridge Presbyterian Church cemetery were probably too young to remember Whitefield's revival message at their church in 1740. All of them, however, would have been familiar with his name and witnessed the impact of his preaching on their community. Just as they knew that they were under the **military authority** of George Washington, it is likely many of those who died at Basking Ridge knew they were under the **spiritual authority** of George Whitefield. Long before the Declaration of Independence, it was Whitefield who preached not only about the new birth in Jesus Christ, but also about the hope that America would become an independent Christian nation, free from bondage to the British crown.

Lessons From the First Great Awakening

We who have inherited the revivalists' legacy need to repent on their behalf for the judgmental spirit of the revivalists who, in their zeal to preach the doctrine of the new birth, forgot that Jesus also taught us not to judge others. This judgmental spirit split apart churches, particularly in places where Whitefield's followers spoke. Jesus' instructions in Luke 10:1–9 provide a key strategy to reach the lost: We are to go into the city and bless the people we meet. If they fail to receive us, we are to kick the dust off our shoes and move on to another place—not to condemn pastors and skeptics who disagree with us theologically. The model of Prayer Evangelism, which we reviewed in Chapter Two, provides a solid foundation for evangelization.

To the extent that Whitefield and his followers failed to follow Jesus' teachings about how to reach a city, they were to some degree responsible for the "dark and threatening clouds" that Edwards saw in New England in 1743. The controversies about unregenerate pastors, the legitimacy of itinerant preachers, and the significance of unusual behavioral manifestations during revival ultimately quenched the work of the Holy Spirit in the First Great Awakening. In short, these controversies plugged up the wells of revival that had caused the Great Awakening to spread rapidly from one community to another.

In order to unplug the wells "which the Philistines had stopped up" (see Genesis 26:18), we must follow in Isaac's footsteps. Just as he returned to the wells his father Abraham had dug, the church today must go back to the ancient wells. We should not expect God to produce new wells of revival until two things happen: First, we must determine what caused the old wells to become plugged up, and second, we must take appropriate steps to remove the stones that are preventing the church from drawing upon the living waters God has so graciously provided for its health and spiritual vitality.

Summary

The Whitefield revivals predated David Brainerd's revivals among the Indians and continued for twenty years after Brainerd's death. Both revivals came out of the Methodist and Puritan heritage of New England, which emphasized the preaching of Knowledge (of scripture) and Fear of the Lord. Thus, both of these awakenings are examples of Type III revivals, as we have defined them in Chapter Two. But Whitefield's revivals, in England as well as in the American Colonies, also included supernatural elements—the projection of his voice to vast audiences, remarkable healings, amazing testimonies of faith by young children, and the like—which indicate that Whitefield was also operating in what Isaiah 11:2 describes as "the Spirit of Counsel and of Power." For this reason, the Whitefield revivals also demonstrated the characteristics of a Type II revival, which became increasingly common in the 20th century as wave after wave of Pentecostal and charismatic revivals spread around the world.

Much of the controversy about the subject of revival, both in Whitefield's day and in subsequent generations, has arisen from the mistaken belief that God always follows the same model in bringing spiritual awakening to His church. Countless arguments and debates among Christians have been caused by our inability "to grasp how wide and long and high and deep is the love of Christ, and to know this love that surpasses knowledge" (Ephesians 3:18–19). *Should it be surprising to us to see that God sent a Type III revival to the American Indians, who were perishing for lack of knowledge of Jesus Christ; but He chose a Type II/III revival for white settlers in the American Colonies, who had heard the gospel message from their parents but had not personally experienced the power of God?* We will return to this topic in Chapter Nine. Before doing so, however, let's see how God visited His people during the Second Great Awakening.

PRAYER

Father, grant me wisdom to learn the lessons of the First Great Awakening. Send me out into the city, as Jesus sent the seventy-two disciples, that I might win men and women to the gospel as a prayer evangelist. Remind me always to bless, fellowship with, and pray for people before presenting the Word of God to them, so that your Kingdom, your power, and your glory will be revealed through my words and actions toward them. Lord, forgive me for being critical of those in Christian leadership who are weaker vessels. Let your winds of revival come again to this region and never again be quenched by disunity in the Body of Christ. Instead, let those who proclaim the Good News be filled not only with the zeal to share the truth but also with the love and grace of Jesus Christ, in whose name I pray. Amen.

CHAPTER SIX

Four Hundred Souls

At Turkey [New Providence] chapel I spoke on 1 Cor. xv,58: it was an open season. When there is a stir amongst the Methodists, other denominations send supplies, if they have not a stationed minister: the process is, to hold a week-day meeting, perform a sacrament or a baptism, to place the new convert within the ark of safety; and all is done. Now we may **stand still,** *or sit still,* **and see the salvation of God!***

—*Francis Asbury's Journal, July 4, 1806*

The next stop on my Highway of Holiness is Interstate 78's Exit 44, located between New Providence and Berkeley Heights. During the Second Great Awakening (1790–1820) these two communities sponsored Methodist camp meetings that attracted spiritually hungry people from many nearby villages. Let's take this exit and find out what happened in these historic wells of revival.

The Hand of God on New Providence

God's hand has been apparent in this area since colonial days. An 1882 historical account states that the first settlers were English, Welsh, and Scottish Presbyterians who were attracted to this area in 1720 by the abundance of wild game in the area. For this reason they called this community "Turkey." The piety of these settlers is noted in this account:

> *These first settlers were religiously educated and inclined. From a record it appears that they not only tilled the land, clearing waste places and making homes for themselves, but held religious meetings prior to the time their first church was established. They were called the Turkey settlement on Long Hill, and went by that name until about the year 1809.*[1]

These original settlers established the Turkey Christian Church in 1737. The second pastor of this congregation was Rev. Azariah Horton, who served them only two years before accepting a call to minister to the Indians on Long Island. It is interesting to note that Horton and David Brainerd were the first two Presbyterian missionaries to the American Indians.

The renaming of the town followed a remarkable event that happened in the year 1759.[2] The author of the 1882 historical account describes this event in the following manner:

The name of the church was changed in 1778 from the Turkey Christian Church to the Presbyterian Church of New Providence, from a circumstance of the escape of the congregation in parts of the gallery giving away. From this event it was considered by the people as a remarkable interposition of Providence for their preservation, and in pious remembrance of it resolved that the church should be called the New Providence Church.[3]

This church experienced a religious revival in 1764, which was part of a national spiritual awakening. The congregation faced many trials during the Revolutionary War and lost forty-eight men in battle. The church building was enlarged in 1782 and was "for a season filled with attentive hearers."[4] By 1803, however, the church suffered from serious "pecuniary embarrassments" and was forced to sell part of the property lying adjacent to the parish. The congregation lost its pastor and had to sell "subscriptions" to meet its financial obligations. By the spring of 1806 the New Providence Presbyterians had been without a pastor for three years and looked with anticipation toward Bishop Francis Asbury's visit to their community.

Asbury's Proclamations

Francis Asbury was said to be the most famous man in America at the turn of the 19th century. He was personally appointed as Methodist Bishop to America by John Wesley and traveled more than 270,000 miles by horseback during the three decades he served as an itinerant minister. Each year he visited every state in the union, and his *Journal* records sixty trips he made through New Jersey during that span of time. It was no wonder that many people considered him to be "The Prophet of the Long Road."[5]

United Methodist Church in New Providence, New Jersey,
which held camp meetings in the first half of the 19ᵗʰ century

Asbury personally commissioned more than four thousand men as Methodist pastors, and he was a shrewd observer of American politics. After he prompted his colleagues to congratulate George Washington for winning the Revolutionary War, the Methodists became the first denomination to endorse the new nation. This politically astute act made headlines in the news media and brought favor to the emerging Methodist movement. He was also a prophet of social change, who denounced liquor and slavery years before mainstream America agreed with his pronouncements on major social issues. He was often seen riding into town with no coat or hat, having given away these clothing items to a needy person at an earlier stop on his preaching circuit.[6]

A Methodist society was founded in New Providence in 1798. In 1802 a powerful revival of religion occurred among the Methodists under the preaching of the Rev. William Mills. The next year

Stephen Day was awakened by the powerful preaching of the Rev. Robert Finley, the Presbyterian pastor from Basking Ridge. Stephen Day was licensed to "preach Methodist" in 1805, and he invited Bishop Asbury to be his house guest in 1806.[7]

In his sermon at the New Providence Methodist Church on the nation's thirtieth birthday (July 4, 1806), Asbury's text was 1 Corinthians 15:58:

> *Therefore, my dear brothers, stand firm. Let nothing move you. Always give yourselves fully to the work of the Lord, because you know that your labor in the Lord is not in vain.*

Even as he spoke these words, Asbury noted that a large number of Presbyterians and unchurched people had come to hear his message, and that there was an unusual receptiveness to the gospel in New Providence. As was noted in the quotation opening this chapter, God was very present in the Methodist weekday meetings Asbury attended. After the local pastor administered a sacrament, there was a large ingathering into the Kingdom of God:

> *Now we may **stand still,** or sit still, **and see the salvation of God!** I rejoiced to hear the appointment of a camp meeting in Turkey in August.*[8]

Asbury's ***Journal*** entry for the next day speaks about the site the Methodists had chosen for their first camp meeting[9] in New Providence and his prayer for a large harvest of souls:

> *The place chosen for the encampment on Turkey I found a handsome height, elegantly sloping to the north. I trust four hundred souls will be converted: may it give new springs and tone to the work of God in the Jerseys!*[10]

In contrast to other New Jersey communities that had resisted the Methodist movement, Asbury found a remarkable unity in the Body of Christ in New Providence. He sensed that the fervor of the Methodist weekday meetings, combined with the willingness of the Presbyterians to "send supplies" to this fledgling society, made it easy for people to come to Jesus Christ in this setting. As Asbury told his eager listeners about camp meetings that were occurring in Kentucky and other states, he prayed and trusted to God that a new awakening would come, which would impact not just New Providence but the entire state of New Jersey. He clearly understood that these religious meetings had the potential to change the spiritual climate of cities and geographic regions.

The Spiritual Climate Changes

A noticeable change in the spiritual climate of New Providence occurred in 1806. The following account describes what happened among the Presbyterians:

> In the spring of 1806, and while the congregation was destitute of any one steadily to break to them the bread of life, it pleased a gracious God in mercy again to visit this church. A spirit of prayer was excited among Christians and a spirit of serious inquiry among the impenitent which continued through the following summer. Mr. Reggs [Rev. Elias Reggs] commenced his labors in the autumn of this year, and had the happiness to see this good-begun work constantly though slowly progressing for more than two years. As a fruit of this gradual but solitary work forty-four were added to the church. Thus the sinking hopes of Zion's friends were revived and their mourning exchanged for joy and thanksgiving.[11]

Presbyterian revivals occurred again in 1813 and 1825, but the latter was short-lived due to the unexpected death of Rev. Reggs that year. Forty-five new members were added to the church in the 1813 awakening and another fourteen in 1825.

Another work of grace occurred at the Presbyterian church beginning in the fall of 1831:

> *In November, 1831, and during the labors of the Rev. Mr. [James] Hynshaw as pastor of this church, the Lord again appeared to revive his people and to build up Zion. The work commenced near the close of a protracted meeting. It was preceded by no very visible tokens of God's presence other than a general solemnity which appeared to pervade the assembly, and a wrestling spirit of prayer on the part of some of God's people. As the protracted service was about to close and the people to retire, "suddenly the spirit of God seemed to descend like a rushing mighty wind and to fill the house where they were sitting." "Men and brethren, what shall we do?" was the instant inquiry of many, while saints, deeply abased, saw with wonder what God had so evidently wrought. As the fruits of this glorious work about thirty were added to the church.* [12]

Impacts of the Camp Meetings

By God's grace both churches in New Providence—the Presbyterian and the Methodist—began to experience spiritual awakenings the year Asbury visited New Providence. If Bishop Asbury's remarks are correct, the unity between these two religious groups was a significant factor in these awakenings. The beginning of the Methodist camp meetings in August 1806, followed by "protracted meetings" among the Presbyterians, must have generated a "sweet, savory offering" to the Lord, to which He responded by allowing many to be saved. The bishop was in frequent contact with the local Methodist church and must have been very pleased by the ingathering of souls in both New Providence churches that year.

Asbury returned to New Providence in 1811 and spoke again on the subject of salvation. In his address in 1898 upon the centennial of Methodism in New Providence, Stephen S. Day (descendant of preacher Stephen Day) gave an account of Asbury's latter visit:

> *A few years later [on May 16, 1811] this privilege was again accorded him, but at this time the Bishop was in very feeble health, so feeble, indeed, that he was obliged to remain seated while preaching. His subject on this occasion was "The Day of Salvation." He urged upon the people the great importance of accepting salvation* **now.** *During the discourse he was often so affected that he would lift his glasses and brush away the tears. Notwithstanding the Bishop's feebleness, he conducted prayers in the family three times a day. After each meal he would say, "Let us pray," and bowing before God, would offer a fervent prayer.*[13]
> [emphasis original]

Day added that the Methodists' fervor and membership continued to grow after Asbury's visits, and they faithfully sponsored annual camp meetings in New Providence and Berkeley Heights during the next fifty years. Day notes that Methodist revivals occurred in these communities in five separate years—1806, 1819, 1824, 1842, and 1858. In the 1824 revival, in particular, so many people were converted in camp meetings in Berkeley Heights that a new Methodist society was formed in that community—the Union Village Church. An even greater awakening occurred in 1842, as Stephen S. Day reported in his 1898 centennial address:

> *In 1842 under the preaching of Mulford Day, New Providence was blessed with probably the greatest revival in its history. Late in the summer a camp meeting was held on Long Hill [between New Providence and Summit], resulting in a number of conversions, but no special interest was apparent. The camp meeting was followed*

by protracted meetings, held on alternate nights at Union Village and New Providence. The meetings were continued for nearly three weeks without any movement on the part of the unconverted. At last two prominent young ladies at the village went forward for prayers and were soundly converted. The next evening one of the converts, Ann Currie Clark, arose from her seat on the ladies' side of the church and passing around to the men's side urged her uncle, a young man and a backslider, again to seek Christ. He refused the invitation, but the noble act of the young lady produced a profound impression, and the next evening about sixty went forward for prayers. From this time the work went like fire in a dry stubble, resulting in 142 probationers at the New Providence Church, and twenty-two at Union Village. Wagon loads of people would come from Union Village to the meetings in New Providence, and the next night wagon loads would go from New Providence to Union Village.[14]

In summary, Francis Asbury introduced the concept of camp meetings to New Providence and began to see the fruits of these meetings before his death in 1816. In contrast to most other communities he visited in New Jersey, he saw that New Providence had a remarkable spiritual climate that could impact the work of God throughout the state. While the success of these camp meetings was apparent through these accounts and by the increases in membership at both the Methodist and Presbyterian congregations, it is interesting to note that none of the five awakenings that occurred during the New Providence camp meeting era produced the harvest of souls that Asbury had been praying for in 1806.

Based on Day's 1898 account, the largest of these five revivals added a combined total of 164 members to the New Providence and Berkeley Heights (Union Village) Methodist congregations. Although precise same-year statistics are not available for the Presbyterian Church at New Providence, it is reasonable to conclude that

Asbury's prayer for four hundred converts in a single year has not yet been answered by the Lord. This being the case, we can take hope in the promise of an even greater revival to come in New Providence and Berkeley Heights, for we read in scripture,

Asbury's prayers for New Providence and Berkeley Heights are still stored up in the golden bowls in heaven, waiting for intercessors in a future generation to come into agreement with his petitions.

Then I saw a Lamb, looking as if it had been slain, standing in the center of the throne, encircled by the four living creatures and the elders. He had seven horns and seven eyes, which are the seven spirits of God sent out into all the earth. He came and took the scroll from the right hand of him who sat on the throne. And when he had taken it, the four living creatures and the twenty-four elders fell down before the Lamb. Each one had a harp and they were holding golden bowls full of incense, which are the prayers of the saints.—Revelation 5:6–8

Although Bishop Asbury's prayer for a harvest of four hundred souls has not yet been answered, this section of scripture causes us to look to the future with expectation. His prayers for New Providence and Berkeley Heights are still stored up in the golden bowls in heaven, waiting for intercessors in a future generation to come into agreement with his petitions.

How Asbury Operated in the Spirit

In Chapters Four and Five we noted that the First Great Awakening was a classic "Type III revival," using the typology developed in Chapter Two. That is to say, based on the Brainerd and Whitefield accounts, revival occurred when the Spirit of the Lord worked together with the Spirit of Knowledge and the Fear of the Lord to cause many individuals to accept Jesus Christ as their Lord and Savior. This same dynamic was present in the New Providence and Berkeley Heights revivals that followed Francis Asbury's visits to this area. Indeed, these New Jersey revivals were very similar to those recorded in western Connecticut between 1797 and 1815.[15]

We see these qualities of Asbury well documented in Ezra Squire Tipple's book, ***Francis Asbury: The Prophet of the Long Road.*** For example, the following quotation describes how he operated in the Spirit of the Lord:

> *Among the contributing causes to the success of the Methodist Evangelism were the men who pressed the battle, men whose zeal was so ardent, whose courage was so audacious, whose devotion was so complete, whose ability to endure hardships and suffering so remarkable, that, like Hercules, whether they rode or prayed or preached, whatever they did, they conquered. There are no more splendid careers in life or literature than those of the early years of American Methodism. While, like Saul, Asbury stands head and shoulders above his brethren, in unconquerable zeal, in passionate energy, in the flaming of a 'divine fire which kept his life incandescent until he dropped at last in the pulpit, consumed by it, or rather borne by it away as if ascending like the Hebrew prophet in a chariot of fire,' he had many worthy comrades. . . . The native preachers of America, men who were born and began their itinerant life in America, cannot be classified. They were not made after a common pattern. 'Herein lies one glory of the early Methodist pioneers—they were individual almost to uniqueness.' . . . What a noble band of heroic souls they were! In thinking of them one scarcely knows where to begin.*[16]

That Asbury operated in the Spirit of Knowledge is clear from the following quotation from Tipple on Methodist preaching:

The earlier preaching of the itinerants was markedly doctrinal. Methodism was not a new theology, but a restatement of the great fundamental truths of the gospel. No other kind of preaching could have produced such marvelous results. I make no claim that these primary truths were preached in a scholastic or scientific manner. Asbury was not a theologian. Neither did his preachers affect to be. They were all too intensely earnest in this business of soul-saving to teach theology or to preach it in an academic fashion. Such a method has always had to give way in all the great revivals of the Christian centuries to another and better method of doctrinal preaching, a method of plain, practical statement and earnest enforcement in direct and pungent appeal to the religious consciousness. The preacher has been the voice of God to warn, to exhort, to persuade. . . .

They had no time to discuss questions of doctrine or to debate mooted questions of theology. 'They entered a village, sounded the alarm, held up the cross, and were gone.' What every preacher tried to do in every sermon was to answer the one great question, What must I do to be saved? Thus he preached God in his infinite holiness and justice and love, and a doctrine of sin most effective in producing the profoundest sense of guilt and peril. The final judgment in the array of its solemnities and issues was heralded in all its awesome imminence and reality. So also was Christ, the Saviour, joyously preached—preached in the fullness of his grace and the pathos of his love. The salvation offered in his name was free and full, and realizable in a present assurance and joyous experience. . . .

Asbury and his associates in the ministry had a royal message to announce to men, a message of life and liberty from God to perishing men. They themselves had experienced the joys of salvation. Not less was their conviction that they were divinely chosen messengers to the people. A ministry with such convictions must be effective. Whoever is believed to have a word from God will find a hearing. Once this fact was established that the Methodist itinerants were bearers of a divine announcement, this in itself was a powerful factor in the extension of the Kingdom. But when was added to this the other fact, that those who heard the announcement and by grace received the gift of God, entered into a joyous Christian experience, and published abroad the joys of the Christian life, and were jealous that others should taste and see, the Church grew by leaps and bounds. [17]

That Asbury operated in the Spirit of the Fear of the Lord is illustrated in the following description, which Tipple attributes to Joshua Marsden:

Many of [Asbury's sermons] were of a nature to strike terror in the hearts of his hearers, and they were meant to do this very thing. Asbury was not like a general watching a dress parade, but as one in the forefront of the fray. He was engaged in stern business. Self-complacency, indifference, unrighteousness were implacable foes, and he used heavy guns and large ammunition, such as:

• *And it shall come to pass at that time, that I will search Jerusalem with candles, and punish the men that are settled on their lees: that say in their heart, The Lord will not do good, neither will he do evil (Zephaniah 1:12).*

• *And whosoever shall fall on this stone shall be broken: but on whomsoever it shall fall, it will grind him to powder (Matthew 21:44).*

• *Then whosoever heareth the sound of the trumpet, and taketh not warning; if the sword come, and take him away, his blood shall be upon his own head (Ezekiel 33:4).*

• *And as it is appointed unto men once to die, but after this the judgment (Hebrews 9:27).*

- *For behold, the day cometh, that shall burn as an oven; and
all the proud, yea, and all that do wickedly, shall be stubble: and
the day that cometh shall burn them up, saith the Lord of hosts,
that it shall leave them neither root nor branch. But unto you that
fear my name shall the [S]un of righteousness arise with healing in
his wings; and ye shall go forth, and grow up as calves of the stall
(Malachi 4:1–2).*
- *The wicked shall be turned into hell, and all the nations that
forget God (Psalms 9:17).*

*These, and others of like portent, formed the ground of appeal to
the fears of men. Knowing the terror of the Lord, he persuaded
thereby. What a distance we have come from that kind of preaching! Sinai no longer belches forth flame and fury. His sons in the
gospel have grown to be milder-mannered men!*[18]

But Asbury's unique gifts went beyond these three spiritual dimensions. His operation in the Spirit of Wisdom is illustrated in the
following passage:

*'He had none of William's wild earnestness; he was without the
charm of Strawbridge or the gentle harmlessness of Richard What-
coat. He had not the thorough humanness of Jesse Lee, nor the
mystical tenderness and strength of Freeborn Garretson.' But in
practical sagacity, love of order, keenness of perception, prompt-
ness of mental actions, shrewd common sense, philosophic imper-
turbability, [and] affable, dignified goodness none of his confreres
surpassed or equaled him.*[19]

How he applied this practical wisdom is described in detail by
Tipple:

*Over and over again Asbury said that no amount of money could
induce him to travel the Long Road; not even 'the wealth of Ormus*

or of Ind' would compensate for the hardships, the sufferings, the perils of the Road. Is it not fortunate that there are some things which bulk larger in a man's life than money? This Republic would have been a different country had Francis Asbury not loved Christ more than Gold.

It was in this formative period of the United States that he traveled the Long Road, and wherever he went he was the prophet of righteousness. He stopped in a thousand homes on the frontiers, and wherever he lodged he lifted men's thoughts to God and instilled ideas of morality. He builded altars in almost every city and town in the United States, and kindled fires thereon which are still burning. He preached the doctrine of human democracy, when the nation was in the midst of a gigantic struggle with paternalism and aristocracy. He inculcated respect for law and order, and created ideals of brotherhood and citizenship along the mountain trails and through the trackless forests where Civilization walked with slow yet conquering step. He challenged despair with the blessed hope of the gospel, and brought to the lonely the companionship of his Christ. He arrested the attention of murderers and blasphemers, halted the reckless in their mad rush after poison-laden pleasures, started crusades against the iniquitous business of the saloon, which have been gathering momentum with every passing year, comforted myriads in their sorrows and agonies, and like a tender, faithful shepherd sought for lost sheep from New Hampshire to the Southern Sea, and from the Atlantic to the Blue Grass lands of Kentucky.[20]

His wisdom, combined with the Spirit of Understanding, allowed him to be an administrative genius without parallel in the 19th century church:

Asbury's relations to his men reveal the secret of his success as an administrator. He seems to have had a marvelous knowledge of men—powers of discrimination that always belong to leaders of men. Boehm in his admirable **Reminiscenses**—*Boehm was for a long time Asbury's traveling companion—says that 'he would sit in Conference and look from under his dark and heavy eyebrows, reading countenances and studying the character and constitution of the preachers, not only for the sake of the Church but for their own sakes. He would say to me: "Henry, Brother A.—or B.—has been too long on the rice plantations, or on the Peninsula. He looks pale; health begins to decline; he must go to the high lands." The preacher would be removed and know not the cause, and the next year come to the Conference with health improved and constitution invigorated.'* [21]

Asbury also operated in the Spirit of Counsel, ever pleading to the Lord for his itinerant pastors and churches:

The authority which he wielded was spiritual. Benjamin M. Adams told me that Aaron Hunt, a distinguished minister of the New York Conference who died in 1858 at the age of ninety years, once said he always knew something hard was coming to him, either a hard circuit or a presiding eldership when Bishop Asbury took him off to pray with him. Ira Ellis recalled many years afterward a prayer of Asbury's at a Conference, when some of the preachers were heard complaining about their all too meager support, and were facing the work and support, or lack of support, of the new Conference year with mutterings of discontent. Listening for a time without rebuke or comment, Bishop Asbury suddenly said, 'Let us pray,' and this is the way he talked with God:

'Lord, we are in thy hands and in thy work. Thou knowest, what is best for us and for thy work, whether poverty or plenty. The hearts of all men are in thy hands. If it is best for us and for thy Church that we should be cramped and straitened, let the people's hands and hearts be closed. If it is better for us—for the

Church—and more to thy glory that we should abound in the
comforts of life, do thou dispose the hearts of those we serve to give
accordingly; and may we learn to be content, whether we abound
or suffer need.'[22]

Another tribute to Asbury's operations in the Spirit of Counsel
is given in the following quotation:

When Washington was inaugurated President, April 30, 1789,
the New York Conference being in session Asbury suggested to it the
propriety of presenting a congratulatory address to the President,
which was done, the duty of reading the address to Washington, at
the meeting arranged for this purpose, devolving upon Asbury. . . .

What an imperial figure is this peerless servant of God! In the
long list of Christian worthies in the heroic age of the republic by
common consent he stands first. There may be some doubt as to
who ranks second, but there can be no debate as to who is chiefest
among them all. Thomas Ware found something in his person, his
piercing eye, his impressive mien, and in the music of his voice
which compelled the attention of all who saw and heard him. He
was a man of commanding power, with interesting and effective
characteristics and strong personal qualities.[23]

Tipple summarizes Asbury's life as a quest for two things: personal holiness and the salvation of the lost:

His Journal is a portraiture of his spiritual aspirations. In my
judgment, no man ever lived who more steadfastly yearned after
holiness than Francis Asbury. Early and late, in log cabins and
beneath the star-flecked sky, in the saddle, and when standing
sentry on a dangerous frontier, everywhere and always, he hun-
gered for holiness. It was one of the two great passions of his
soul—personal holiness—the other, and greater even, being the
salvation and sanctification of other precious souls.[24]

By his words and deeds, Francis Asbury left an eternal legacy in New Providence, Berkeley Heights, and thousands of other American communities. He paved the way for later revivals based on the Spirit of Wisdom and Understanding (Type I) and the Spirit of Counsel and Power (Type II). The Methodist Holiness movement, for example, was an outgrowth of Methodism that originated in Vineland, New Jersey, in 1867. It resulted in the launch of more than twenty-five new religious groups (including the Nazarenes and various Brethren groups) and was an antecedent of the charismatic renewal revivals in the 20th century. With their emphasis on gifts of prophecy, tongues, miracles of faith, and so on, these are examples of Type II revivals.

As we continue along my Highway of Holiness, we will discover that a classic Type I revival occurred in New York City half a century after Asbury's first visit to New Providence. So let's continue traveling east on I-78 and see what a revival based on the Spirit of Wisdom and Understanding looks like.

PRAYER

Lord, we know that your hand is on us every day. Grant that we might see your works of providence before us and remember your great deeds from the past. We believe that the unfulfilled prayer requests of past generations are still stored in golden bowls of incense in heaven, and we come into agreement with our forefathers for the fulfillment of these requests. We thank you for unity in the Body of Christ and how you honor that unity by revealing your divine presence on earth. We pray that the church, filled anew with the fear and admonition of the Lord, will continue to advance your Kingdom in our region. In Jesus' name we pray. Amen.

CHAPTER SEVEN

Jeremiah Lanphier Calls
a Prayer Meeting

No man there, no man perhaps, living or dead, has ever seen any thing like it. On the day of Pentecost, Peter preached; Luther preached; and Livingston, Wesley, and Whitefield! Great spiritual movements have been usually identified with some eloquent voice. But no name, except the Name that is above every name, is identified with this Meeting.

—*Rev. Talbot W. Chambers,* **The New York City Noon Prayer Meeting**[1]

The fourth and final stop on my Highway of Holiness is New York City. In 1857 a revival broke out that was completely different from earlier spiritual awakenings in America. Let's conclude our Highway of Holiness journey by checking out what happened that year at the North Dutch Reformed Church in Lower Manhattan.

Revival broke out at the North Dutch Reformed Church in New York City in 1857. Photo by permission of the Collection of the New-York Historical Society, negative number 78267d.

How the Noon Prayer Meetings Began

When God wants to bring revival to a nation, He often raises up great leaders to inspire the people. In the First Great Awakening He used men like Jonathan Edwards, the Wesleys, George White-field, Gilbert Tennent, and David Brainerd to preach to the people in colonial America. Prominent preachers during the Second Great Awakening included Francis Asbury, Edward Dorr Griffin, Asahel Nettleton, Lyman Beecher, Charles Finney, and many capable leaders from the "New Divinity School" at Yale. These men were gifted orators who taught the Scriptures with passion and urged their listeners to accept Jesus Christ before their souls perished under divine judgment.

But the Third Great Awakening, which began in the fall of 1857, had a distinctly different spiritual dynamic. In 1856 a Methodist named William Arthur published a book of sermons that concluded with a prayer pleading with God to "Crown this nineteenth century with a revival of pure and undefiled religion . . . greater than any demonstration of the Spirit ever vouchsafed to man."[2] Rev. Arthur's prayer was soon answered.

The North Dutch Reformed Church ministered to the spiritual needs of the increasingly diverse population who lived and worked in Lower Manhattan. While the church was filled to capacity during the first decades of the 19th century, by 1857 the Sunday worship attendance had declined precipitously. Meanwhile, immigrants were streaming into New York from all over Europe and Asia, many of whom had no church background. In response to this situation, the board of the North Dutch Reformed Church devised an evangelistic outreach plan to increase interest and participation in the divine Word in Lower Manhattan.

In June of 1857 the board hired a forty-six-year-old businessman named Jeremiah C. Lanphier to direct this community outreach program. One news correspondent described Lanphier as "tall, with a pleasant face, an affectionate manner, indomitable energy and perseverance, a good singer, gifted in prayer and exhortation, a welcome guest to any house, shrewd and endowed with much tact and common sense."[3] Although he had never done this type of work, he resigned from his position in the mercantile industry to become a full-time evangelist on July 1, 1857. Samuel Prime recounts how Lanphier approached God about his new assignment:

> *In the upper lecture-room of the 'Old North Dutch Church', in*
> *Fulton Street, New York, a solitary man was kneeling upon the*

floor, engaged in earnest, importunate prayer. He was a man who lived very much in the lives of others; lived almost wholly for others. He had no wife or children—but there were thousands with their husbands and fathers, without God and hope in the world; and these thousands were going to the gates of eternal death. He had surveyed all the lower wards of the city as a lay-missionary of the Old Church, and he longed to do something for their salvation. He knew he could do many things—he could take tracts in his hand, any and every day, and distribute them. He could preach the gospel from door to door. All this he had done. To reach these perishing thousands, he needed a thousand lives. Could not something more effectual be done? So, day after day, and many times a day, this man was on his knees, and his constant prayer was 'Lord, what wilt thou have me to do?' The oftener he prays, the more earnest he becomes. He pleads with God to show him what to do, and how to do it. . . . But though he prayed and believed, he had not the remotest idea of the methods of God's grace which were about to be employed. The more he prayed, however, the more confident he became that God would show him what he would have him to do.[4]

> **Day after day, and many times a day, Jeremiah Lanphier was on his knees, and his constant prayer was, "Lord, what wilt thou have me to do?"**

One day, as Lanphier was making his rounds on the streets of Lower Manhattan, the idea for a noon prayer meeting came to his mind. He describes this moment of inspiration in his journal:

Going my rounds in the performance of my duty one day, as I was walking along the streets, the idea was suggested to my mind that an hour of prayer, from twelve to one o'clock, would be beneficial *to business men, who usually in great numbers take that hour for rest and refreshment. The idea was to have singing, prayer, exhortation, relation of religious experience, as the case might be; that none should be required to stay the whole hour; that all should come and go as their engagements should allow or require, or their inclinations dictate. Arrangements were made, and at twelve o'clock noon, on the 23*rd* day of September, 1857, the door of the third storey lecture-room was thrown open. At half-past twelve the step of a solitary individual was heard upon the stairs. Shortly after another, and another; then another, and last of all, another, until six made up the whole company! We had a good meeting. The Lord was with us to bless us.*[5]

Lanphier was encouraged by this first meeting and scheduled the second meeting for the following Wednesday, September 30. The attendance increased from six to twenty, and he reports that it was "a precious meeting. There was much prayer, and the hearts of those present were melted within them."[6] The third meeting, on October 7, had between thirty and forty attendees and was so animated that they decided to hold another meeting the very next day. This started the first of the "businessmen's union daily prayer-meetings." By October 14 the noon prayer meetings at the Fulton Street church were drawing more than one hundred attendees. Lanphier's journal entry for that day states,

Over one hundred present, many of them not professors of religion, but under conviction of sin, and seeking an interest in Christ; inquiring what they shall do to be saved. God grant that they find Christ precious to their souls.[7]

Lanphier distributed handbills about the noon prayer meeting throughout the Financial District and published the following set of rules about how the meetings were to be conducted:

1. The leader is not expected to exceed ten minutes in opening the meeting. Open the meeting by reading and singing from three to five verses of a hymn.

2. Prayer.

3. Read a portion of the Scripture.

4. Say the meeting is now open for prayers and exhortations, observing particularly the rules overhead, inviting brethren from abroad to take part in the services.

5. Read but one or two requests at a time—REQUIRING a prayer to follow—such prayer to have special reference to the same.

6. In case of any suggestion or proposition by any person, say that this is simply a Prayer meeting, and that they are out of order, and call on some brother to pray.

7. Give out the closing hymn five minutes before one o'clock. Request the Benediction from a Clergyman, if one be present.[8]

The Noon Prayer Meetings picked up greater intensity after the New York Stock Exchange crashed on October 13, 1857. Five months after the market crash, 10,000 people gathered for noon prayer in New York City alone. Other churches and theaters began to sponsor prayer meetings, and all these rooms filled up almost as quickly as they opened. By now the prayer meetings had gained the attention of the popular press. The New York **Herald** and New York **Tribune** both devoted an entire issue to the prayer meetings early in 1858, and several widely circulated journals began publishing "the Progress of the Revival" as a featured column.

Although the financial crisis undoubtedly increased interest in the Noon Prayer Meetings, these meetings were well under way before the market collapsed. As Samuel Prime noted, the underlying cause of the prayer meetings was a renewed interest in prayer among God's people. He writes,

When we come to the history of the third month of prayer, what a change we find rapidly taking place, not only in the city, but all over the land. It was everywhere a revival of prayer. It was not prayer-meetings in imitation of the Fulton Street meetings. Those that say so, or think so, greatly err. God was preparing his glorious way over the nation. It was the desire to pray. The same Power that moved to prayer in Fulton Street, moved to prayer elsewhere. The same characteristics that marked the Fulton Street meeting, marked all similar meetings. The Spirit of the Lord was poured out upon these assemblages, and it was this that made the places of prayer all over the land places of great solemnity, and earnest inquiry. Men did not doubt—could not doubt—that God was moving in answer to prayer. It was this solemn conviction that silenced all opposition—that awakened the careless and stupid—that encouraged and gladdened the hearts of Christians—causing a general turning to the Lord. Such a display of love and mercy, on the part of the ever blessed Spirit, was never made before. The religious press, all over the country, heralded the glad news of what the Lord was doing in some places; thus preparing the way for what he was about to do in others. Thousands on thousands of closets bore witness to strong crying and tears before God in prayer all over the land. Thousands of waiting hearts, hearing that Jesus was passing by, begged that he would tarry long enough to look on them. [9]

The Prayer Meetings Spread Across the U.S.

From Manhattan the Noon Prayer Meetings quickly spread to Brooklyn, Newark, Jersey City, Philadelphia, and many other cities across the United States. During the winter of 1858 businessmen's prayer meetings were established in all parts of the land—including Boston, Baltimore, Washington, Richmond, Charleston, Savannah, Mobile, New Orleans, Vicksburg, Memphis, St. Louis, Pittsburgh,

Cincinnati, Chicago, and numerous other cities. Prime describes how the prayer meetings impacted American life in a matter of a few weeks:

> *The northern, middle, western, and southern States were moved as by one common mighty influence. The spirit of the revival spread everywhere, and seemed to permeate every nook and corner of the great republic. The subjects of the revival included all classes—the high and the low—the rich and the poor—the learned and the ignorant. The most hopeless and forbidding were brought under its almighty power. From the highest to the lowest and most degraded in society, the trophies of God's power and grace were made. Persons of the most vicious and abandoned character, supposed to be beneath and beyond the reach of all religious influence, by having lost all susceptibility, were brought to humble themselves like little children at the foot of the cross. Christians were themselves astonished and overwhelmed at those displays of divine mercy. They felt that God was saying to them, anew, and by a providential revelation—'Before they call, I will answer, and while they are yet speaking, I will hear.' 'Open thy mouth wide, and I will fill it.' Christians became emboldened to ask great things and expect great things. Never before, in modern times certainly, was there such asking in prayer—such believing in prayer, and never such answers to prayer.*
>
> *The spectacle of such universal confidence in God was without a parallel. It appeared in all prayers. It appeared in all addresses. It appeared in all conversations. It spread from heart to heart. There was humility, and yet there was a cheerful, holy boldness in the spirit and temper of the religious mind, and duty was attempted with the expectation of success. It seemed to be upon all hearts as if written with the pen of a diamond—'My soul! wait thou only upon God, for my expectation is from him.'*[10]

The Spirit of the Lord seemed to hang over the land, and this presence extended from land out into the eastern seas. Ships on the Atlantic Ocean approaching the U.S. began to feel the influence of the revival while they were still one hundred miles east of New York City, and dozens of ocean liners reported that their crews and passengers had been seized with a conviction of sin and turned to Christ before reaching port.[11] Another commentator noted the impact of the revival on enlisted sailors:

> *Ships coming into New York Harbor came under the power of God's presence. On one ship a captain and thirty men were converted to Christ before the ship docked. Four sailors knelt for prayer down in the depths of the battleship North Carolina anchored in the harbor. They began to sing and their ungodly shipmates came running down to make fun, but the power of God gripped them and they humbly knelt in repentance.*[12]

Worldwide Impacts

By May of 1859 more than 50,000 men and women in the Northeast had come to Christ through the prayer revival. Across the United States, more than 1 million unchurched people had accepted Jesus Christ by the end of the revival in 1859. Leaders such as D. L. Moody and Phoebe Palmer launched evangelistic campaigns that continued for decades after the revival ended.

Meanwhile, the move of God's Spirit spread internationally. In September 1857, just as Lanphier was beginning the New York prayer meetings, a young Irishman named James McQuilkin began a prayer meeting in Ulster with three other men. Other Irishmen began similar prayer meetings, and by 1859 more than 100,000 people in Ireland became converts and joined the churches. Similar revivals broke out in England, Scotland, and Wales, adding more than 1 million to the church rolls in these countries within two years.[13]

In London Charles Haddon Spurgeon gave a whole year of revival sermons at Surrey Gardens Music Hall in 1859. As he watched the revival spread from New York to Ulster to England, crowds of up to eight thousand per day heard him preach about the great work of God in that season of spiritual awakening.[14] One hundred years later the Rev. Martyn Lloyd-Jones delivered twenty-four sermons on the subject of the 1859 revival. In the first of these messages, entitled "The Urgent Need for Revival Today," Lloyd-Jones described why the present church needs to understand the subject of revival:

> [I]t happens to be the year 1959, a year in which many will be calling to mind and celebrating the great revival, the great religious awakening, the unusual outpouring and manifestation of the Spirit of God, that took place one hundred years ago, in 1859. In that year there was a revival, first in the United States of America, and afterwards in Northern Ireland, in Wales and parts of Scotland, and even in certain parts of England, and this year there are many who will be calling this to mind and commemorating that great and signal movement of the Spirit of God. I believe it is right that we should participate in this, and understand why it is being done, and why the Church of God should be very concerned about it at this present juncture. This is obviously a matter for the whole Church and not merely for certain of her leaders. The history of revivals brings out that very clearly, for God often acts in a most unusual manner, and produces revival and keeps it going, not necessarily through ministers but perhaps through people who may have regarded themselves as very humble and unimportant members of the Christian Church.[15]

The Prayer Meetings and the Holy Spirit

So what was the cause of such an extraordinary movement of God? Part of the answer is surely the humble, obedient heart of Jeremiah Lanphier as he prayed for the lost in New York. Another part of the answer is undoubtedly the prayer meetings themselves, which created an atmosphere of "open heavens" throughout the entire New York region. And the desperate economic situation, combined with the attention the media gave to the prayer meetings, certainly helped to fan the flames of revival throughout the United States and around the world.

Every weekday, visitors from other areas and nations would attend the New York prayer meetings or send personal prayer requests. Everyone, it seemed, knew that the Spirit of the Lord was very present in New York City, and people came to expect answers to their prayer petitions and meaning in this tumultuous time in American history.

The following quotation from Samuel Prime helps to shed light on the spiritual dynamics of this great revival:

Let us for a moment look at some of those passages of Scripture which were the subjects of discourses during the period of which we have been speaking, and see how remarkable they are. They are the foundations of sermons, by a great number of preachers, selected without any preconcert, and distinctly show how the minds of these ambassadors of the Lord Jesus were led. They are the texts of sermons which have never been published, but delivered during this period in the Old Dutch Church:

• 1 Corinthians 1:30–31: 'But of him are ye in Christ Jesus, who of God is made unto us wisdom, and righteousness, and sanctification, and redemption; that according as it is written, he that glorieth, let him glory in the Lord.'

- *1 Corinthians 10:16 [sic; 10:15]: 'I speak as to wise men; judge ye what I say.'*
- *Psalm 30:6,7: 'And in my prosperity I said, I shall never be moved. Lord! by thy favor thou didst make my mountain to stand strong. Thou didst hide thy face, and I was troubled.'*
- *Psalm 17:5: 'Hold up my goings in thy paths, that my footsteps slip not.'*[16]

From these passages and the rest of what has been said in previous pages, is it not clear that the 1857–59 prayer revival was one in which the Spirit of the Lord operated together with the Spirit of Wisdom and Understanding? As businessmen and -women met together for prayer every day, they came to the Lord searching for practical answers to troubling life problems—unsaved friends and family members, a loss of job and/or career, and a world in which all they pursued paled in comparison with the awesome presence and greatness of God.

As Martyn Lloyd-Jones pointed out, occasionally God uses men of no reputation at all as agents of mighty revivals. Such were the revivals of 1857–59 in the United States, Ulster, and many other nations. Sometimes it takes a no-name person such as Jeremiah Lanphier or James McQuilkin to break through the clouds of darkness. As Isaiah wrote some 2,500 years ago, we should not be surprised to find that God uses humble people to build up Highways of Holiness:

> *"Build up, build up, prepare the road! Remove the obstacles out of the way of my people." For this is what the high and lofty One says—he who lives forever, whose name is holy: "I live in a high and holy place, but also with him who is contrite and lowly in spirit, to revive the spirit of the lowly and to revive the heart of the contrite."* —*Isaiah 57:14–15*

Should we, then, be surprised to find that the next great revival in New York City might be led by unheralded businesspeople similar to Jeremiah Lanphier, people whose great passion in life is that the Kingdom of God be advanced as they pray to build up the Highways of Holiness that God has revealed to them?

PRAYER

O God, as I walk around my city, neighborhood, or workplace, let me not be discouraged and confused by the tumult around me. Grant me to hear your still, small voice each day as I ask, "Lord, what wilt thou have me to do?" And as I continue to seek your will in prayer, give me ever-increasing confidence to implement the strategy that you reveal to me in the prayer closet. Father, I thank you that you are willing to use no-name individuals like me to advance your Kingdom. Let me not be concerned about how large my ministry is or what others think of me. Only grant me the ability to pray for men and women and lead them into the Kingdom according to your perfect timing and purposes. In Jesus' precious name I pray. Amen.

PART THREE

Your Highway of Holiness

CHAPTER EIGHT

Preparing Your Highway of Holiness

We live in a day wherein God is doing marvelous things: in that respect, we are distinguished from former generations. God has wrought great things in New England, which though exceedingly glorious, have all along been attended with some threatening clouds, which, from the beginning, caused me to apprehend some great stop or check to be put to the work, before it should be begun and carried on its genuine purity and beauty, to subdue all before it, and to prevail with an irresistible and continual progress and triumph; and it is come to pass according to my apprehensions. But yet I cannot think otherwise, than that what he has now been doing, is the forerunner of something vastly greater, more pure, and more extensive. . . . I believe God will not wholly cease till it has subdued the whole earth.

—*Jonathan Edwards,* **Memoirs,** *Chapter XII, p. cxiv*

But Lord, Aren't There Other Highways?

After contemplating what God had done at the "wells of revival" described in Chapters Four through Seven, I realized that I had only

begun to describe all the marvelous revivals that have touched New
Jersey since colonial times. I hadn't even mentioned the spiritual
awakenings that occurred in Newark, Elizabeth, Woodbridge,
Princeton, Trenton, Atlantic City, Salem, Deerfield, Jackson, and
dozens of other cities in the Garden State. And I'd said nothing at all
about the past awakenings in other states and nations. I began to
question whether I had chosen the right path for the Highway of
Holiness.

In a troubled moment I cried out, "But Lord, aren't there other
Highways of Holiness?" And almost as soon as I completed my
prayer, a feeling of peace came over me. "Yes, there are," was the
thought that came to my mind, "but it will be up to others to discover their own Highway of Holiness."

> **"But Lord, aren't there other Highways of Holiness?"**
>
> **"Yes, there are, but it will be up to others to discover their own Highway of Holiness."**

Before we describe how to do this, let's stop to consider what the Bible says about the Highway of Holiness.

What Is a Highway of Holiness?

The first reference to this concept is found in Isaiah 35. We
mentioned this section of scripture at the end of Chapter Three but
did not define precisely what a "Highway of Holiness" is. So now
let's consider this concept in greater detail.

In Isaiah 35:8–10 we read,

> *And a highway will be there; it will be called the Way of Holiness.
> The unclean will not journey on it; it will be for those who walk in
> that Way; wicked fools will not go about on it. No lion will be
> there, nor will any ferocious beast get up on it; they will not be*

*found there. But only the redeemed will walk there, and the ran-
somed of the LORD will return. They will enter Zion with singing;
everlasting joy will crown their heads. Gladness and joy will over-
take them, and sorrow and sighing will flee away.*

One commentator (J. A. Motyer) summarizes this passage of
scripture in the following manner:

> But let us concentrate for a moment on the **highway** of verse 8. It
> is the way to everlasting joy. It is the way to Zion, the city of God,
> and all that it symbolizes. In New Testament terms it is the high-
> way to heaven. And it is **the Way of Holiness,** which puts us in
> touch again with a major theme of the book [of Isaiah]. For Isai-
> ah, holiness is the defining characteristic of God himself. Above all
> else, God is holy (6:3), so the way of holiness is not just the way to
> Zion, or the way to heaven; it is the way to God. It is not the
> golden streets or the pearly gates that make heaven what it is, but
> the presence of God. To be in heaven is to be with God for ever, in
> totally joyous, unspoiled fellowship. And the way to heaven is pro-
> vided by God himself. It is for those who have been **redeemed,** or
> ransomed (9–10). They have their roots in the exodus from Egypt,
> and find their final significance in the work of Christ, by which
> God rescues us from the power of sin and Satan. These acts of
> judgment and deliverance are the expressions, **par excellence,** of
> his holiness. Look at them, and you will see his holiness in action.
> The way of holiness is the way of salvation that God provides.[1]

**This commentary on Isaiah 35:8 clearly demonstrates that
this highway, the "Way of Holiness," is the path of salvation
that takes believers to Zion.** We find descriptions of Zion in
several passages of scripture, including verses in the Book of Psalms,
the prophecies of Zechariah, and John's vision in Revelation 21. If
this were all the Bible said about the Way of Holiness, we might

think that God will do all the work to build this highway, and that our job is simply to gain access to this road by developing personal habits of holiness. Under this scenario we could imagine that a lot of people would be interested in becoming monks—possibly even hermit monks—so they would not face the trials and temptations of this fallen world.

But Isaiah doesn't stop with this description of the "Way of Holiness" in chapter 35. In chapter 61 he tells us there will be a Year of the Lord's Favor, during which the people of God will restore the ruined places. Specifically, Isaiah tells us that in the Year of the Lord's favor,

> *They will rebuild the ancient ruins and restore the places long devastated; they will renew the ruined cities that have been devastated for generations. Aliens will shepherd your flocks; foreigners will work your fields and vineyards. And you will be called priests of the LORD, you will be named ministers of our God. You will feed on the wealth of nations, and in their riches you will boast. Instead of their shame my people will receive a double portion, and instead of disgrace they will rejoice in their inheritance; and so they will inherit a double portion in their land, and everlasting joy will be theirs.* —Isaiah 61:4–7

When Jesus read the beginning of Isaiah 61 in the synagogue at Nazareth (as described in Luke 4:16–19), He not only proclaimed the Year of the Lord's favor, but also made a significant addition as recorded in Luke 4:21:

> *"Today this scripture is fulfilled in your hearing."*

Now that Jesus has been raised from the dead and ascended into heaven, He has left with us the same Holy Spirit that was upon Him, under whose authority we are commissioned to "rebuild the ancient ruins and restore the places long devastated." Because of the anointing of the Spirit in each believer, we have become "priests of the Lord" and "ministers of our God." These verses, in conjunction with Revelation 1:6, tell us that we have become "a kingdom and priests" to restore the places that have been desolate for generations. These are also foundational verses for understanding the new marketplace transformation movement that has been described by Ed Silvoso, Rich Marshall, and other writers.[2]

If the Holy Spirit is now present to empower us for the necessary job of restoration, what must we do to begin this work? Let's consider two answers to this question. First, in Isaiah 62:6–7 we read,

> *I have posted watchmen on your walls, O Jerusalem; they will never be silent day or night. You who call on the LORD, give yourselves no rest, and give him no rest till he establishes Jerusalem and makes her the praise of the earth.*

In other words, it's up to the watchmen—or intercessors, as we call them today—to ceaselessly call out to God to supply the spiritual resources needed to complete the restoration of Jerusalem, which represents the present dwelling place of God on earth, regardless of geographic location. In the next section we will see that God gives very specific directions about how today's "marketplace ministers" are to build Highways of Holiness on earth.

The second thing we must do to begin this process of restoration is to identify how the church has quenched past moves of the Holy Spirit in our area. Chuck Pierce provided a major key to New Jersey intercessors in his message to the New Jersey Strategic Prayer Network (now the New Jersey Global Apostolic Prayer Network) on August 21, 2002. A portion of this message is given below:

New Jersey has been under a shadow. It is time for the shadow of darkness that has been over New Jersey to begin to lift. Matter of fact, when you start trying to find out about New Jersey, you usually get led to New York. New York overshadows New Jersey in a lot of things that are going on. But yet, God is bringing New Jersey and the Body of Christ into its identity at this time. A shadow is a dark image or object that interrupts rays of light. And He said there had been various images in the state that had interrupted Him rending the heaven and coming down.

He told me very specifically there had been four distinct times in this state when He has attempted to remove the shadow over New Jersey and come and dwell in your midst. You'll have to go back and have to look at the history of that and find out when that has been. And he said because of that, a shadow has networked together. So not only is He going to erect the pillars throughout the state that can begin to raise the anointing level over the state, but I actually see you participating on the four borders of the state, North, South, East, West, to declare/repent of what has come into the state that has quenched His Spirit. Now hear me, not the injustices of what has happened with people, but when His Spirit has tried to visit and as a people you have rejected His Spirit. So many times we are looking at who has done what to whom, whether it is Native American, blacks, whites, you know, God is going to work all of that out of us. But He is saying it is more important now "when I have tried to visit and you have rejected Me." And He said very specifically there was a shadow upon this state at times when He had come to visit and you have not received Him. He is ready to remove it. And every time you do this, what is going to happen is, light is going to flood in. You're going to feel His presence coming in.[3]

Approach to Manhattan via U.S. 3 in Nutley, New Jersey

How to Prepare Your Highway of Holiness

Isaiah further describes in chapter 62 the highway we are to build:

> *Pass through, pass through the gates! Prepare the way for the people. Build up, build up the highway! Remove the stones. Raise a banner for the nations. The LORD has made proclamation to the ends of the earth: "Say to the Daughter of Zion, 'See, your Savior comes! See, his reward is with him, and his recompense accompanies him.'" They will be called the Holy People, the Redeemed of the LORD; and you will be called Sought After, the City No Longer Deserted.* —Isaiah 62:10–12

This passage implies that the proclamation is not for only one highway or one people group but is for *all* the nations. In addition, it gives us several important instructions about how we are to prepare these Highways of Holiness.

1. Get Moving

Isaiah tells us that we must begin by taking a very specific action, namely ***passing through.*** This phrase is reminiscent of God's instruction to Moses in Exodus 14:15–16, when He told the leader of Israel to cross from dry land into the Red Sea. The people of Israel were clearly in a desperate state, with Pharaoh's army behind them and a large body of water in front of them. When Moses believed that what was humanly impossible could happen, he lifted his staff, the waters parted, and the people of Israel crossed over the Red Sea to safety.

A similar thing happened to Joshua when he reached the Jordan River some forty years later. The people of Israel had been hoping to receive the Promised Land for generations, and now in Joshua chapter 3 we read that only a body of water separated them from the land promised to them. Yet they had reason to fear the obstacles they faced. In the first place, the Jordan River was at flood stage, and they lacked boats to get across. But even if they crossed safely, they would surely face opposition from the inhabitants of Canaan. Under these circumstances, the natural human tendency would have been to settle where they were on the east side of the River.

And isn't this where the church is today? As we look at the divided state of the evangelical church, and consider the broken cities before us, don't we just want to settle in where we are rather than battling for something we can't presently see?

That's why Isaiah tells us that our first step is to ***pass through.*** We aren't to be satisfied with where we are. We can't fulfill God's will by driving in neutral. When God gives us spiritual gifts, they are not intended to make us feel good about ourselves. Instead, they are provided so we can move out into unknown territory and there advance the Kingdom of God.

2. Pass Through the Gates

Moreover, this passage tells us that we are to pass through the **gates.** When we come to a foreign land, there are only two ways for us to enter. We can either advance to the gate and enter legally, or alternatively "jump the fence" and come in without legal permission. If we choose the first course of action, we can be sure the legal authorities will be aware of our entry as we seek their approval (while risking their denial). But if we choose to "jump the fence," then we will surely face opposition and punishment when the officials find out we have entered their area illegally.

In John 10:1–3 Jesus tells us that those who follow Him must choose the first alternative:

> *"I tell you the truth, the man who does not enter the sheep pen by the gate, but climbs in by some other way, is a thief and a robber. The man who enters by the gate is the shepherd of his sheep. The watchman opens the gate for him, and the sheep listen to his voice. He calls his own sheep by name and leads them out."*

Those of us who claim a European heritage have much to learn from First Nations people in regard to the importance of protocol. Dr. Suuqiina, an Inuit evangelist from Alaska, makes this point clear in his book, *Can You Feel the Mountains Tremble? A Healing the Land Handbook:*

> *When a First Nations person traveled into other tribal territories, certain kinds of protocol were practiced. The reason being that the traveler did not possess authority upon the land in the same way or to the same degree as those living on the land. The traveler would seek permission to travel, camp, hunt, or trade within the territory. This permission was sought from the highest authority in the land, the chief, who was the gatekeeper of that nation or tribe.*

> *An audience with the chief would be sought, the mission stat-*
> *ed, the length of stay, gifts and honors exchanged, and permission*
> *granted or withheld by the gatekeeper. With permission the immi-*
> *grant possessed a new measure of authority, not "taken" but "gift-*
> *ed," to proceed to the desired destination.*[4]

This passage reminds us that there are only two ways we can move into a new area: We will come either like a shepherd or like a thief. If our goal is to model the life of Jesus, the "Good Shepherd," then we must enter through the gate like a shepherd. If we fail to follow the gatekeeper's protocol, we run the risk of being appre- hended as a thief. By following established protocol, however, we deny the enemy an opportunity to quench our efforts and malign our character.

3. Prepare the Way for the People

After we enter the gates of the city, our next step is to prepare the way for the Kingdom of God to come to the people. Many city- dwellers today are broken people, for a variety of reasons. We cannot win the people to Jesus Christ unless we are able to achieve reconciliation among these hurting brothers and sisters. By operat- ing in the authority of a peacemaker, we push back darkness and open paths of hope to city dwellers who are leading lives of despera- tion.

In his book *Anointed for Business,* Ed Silvoso identifies six types of reconciliation, or peacemaking, that Paul mentions in his letter to the Ephesians:

- **Ethnic** (Ephesians 2:13–22) — People of different ethnic backgrounds need to be "built together into a dwell- ing of God in the Spirit" (2:22).

- **Denominational** (Ephesians 3:16–21) — When saints are rooted and grounded in love, the love of God causes them to be "filled up to all the fullness of God" (3:19).
- **Ministerial** (Ephesians 4:1–6) — All are exhorted to "preserve the unity of the Spirit in the bond of peace" (4:3).
- **Gender** (Ephesians 5:21–33) — This passage teaches how to bridge the division between men and women through mutual submission (5:21), which leads to unconditional love on the part of husbands and unlimited respect on the part of wives (5:33).
- **Generational** (Ephesians 6:1–4) — This is a reference to the reconciling work of Christ between fathers and children (see also Malachi 4:6).
- **Marketplace** (Ephesians 6:5–9) — Paul describes how masters and slaves are to be bonded together by the love of Jesus Christ, their common master. This removes the widest human gap that exists in the marketplace.[5]

Silvoso points out that bringing resolution in these areas of conflict allows God's people to "be strong in the Lord" (Ephesians 6:10) and stand against the forces of wickedness, having "put on the full armor of God" (Ephesians 6:11). Note that part of the armor includes having our "feet fitted with the readiness that comes from the gospel of peace" (Ephesians 6:15).

It is significant to note that Jonathan Edwards also touched on the theme of marketplace reconciliation in his reflections on the First Great Awakening of 1734–42. In the following passage he notes that deeds of charity toward the poor are essential during a period in which Christians sense the imminent arrival of a spiritual awakening:

At a time when there is an apparent approach of any glorious re-
vival of God's church, he especially calls his people to the practice
of moral duties (Isaiah 41:1): "Thus saith the Lord, Keep ye
judgment, and do justice; for my salvation is near to come, and my
righteousness to be revealed." So when John preached that "the
Kingdom of heaven is at hand," and cried to the people, "Prepare
ye the way of the Lord, make his paths straight," (Luke 3:4), the
people answered him, "What they should do?" He answers, "He
that hath two coats, let him impart to him who has none, and he
that hath meat, let him do likewise. . . ." God's people at such
time as this, ought especially to abound in deeds of charity, or
alms-giving.[6]

4. Build Up the Highway

The purpose of a highway is to facilitate the movement of people between different cities and villages. As we saw in Chapters
Four through Seven, all of these great revivals of the past moved
from community to community through itinerant preachers and
marketplace ministers. After a spark of revival broke out in one
community, the revival spread and intensified as it extended to
surrounding communities. To the extent that geographical isolation
and fragmentation between communities is a barrier to a move of
God, building up the highway increases the number of people who
can readily participate in a move of God. Moreover, building up the
highway is a positive act that believers can take in order "that the
King of glory may come in" (Psalm 24:7).

5. Remove the Stones

Next, Isaiah 62 exhorts us to clear away the stones that impede
travel on the highway. The highway may be in perfect condition,
but it must be cleared of rubble to facilitate travel. This verse is

reminiscent of Genesis 26:18, which tells us that Isaac had to redig Abraham's wells, which the Philistines had clogged up with stones.

Roads in disrepair certainly create problems of safety and aesthetics but may also cause shame and demoralize the people. Removing the stones not only opens up wells and highways but also removes hidden obstacles (shame, fear, feelings of victimization, and so on) that can impede the advancement of the Kingdom of God in a community or neighborhood.

6. Raise a Banner for the Nations

Psalm 96:3 tells us that we are to "Declare [God's] glory among the nations, his marvelous deeds among all peoples." When we praise God and intercede for other nations and people groups, we come into agreement with God's purpose to gather all believers together in the New Jerusalem, as John describes in Revelation 21. Many missionaries and "ambassadors of Christ" who regularly intercede on behalf of other nations have noted that these prayers often have more power than their prayers for personal or local concerns. God seems to have a strong passion to break down barriers across nations, as evidenced by the dramatic answers to prayer that often occur when Christians pray across national boundaries.

Raising a banner for the nations is also part of God's plan for unstopping wells of revival. As we redig stopped-up wells, God honors our faithfulness by opening new wells of living water (see Genesis 26:32). These new wells have the potential to meet the needs of others who are thirsty. The concept of wells of revival reminds us that God is always concerned about providing living water to *all* who thirst, not simply meeting our *individual* needs.

7. See, Your Savior Comes

In Chapter Two we described the model of Prayer Evangelism[7], which is based on Luke 10:1–9 and the four steps Jesus instructs His disciples to follow (bless, fellowship, pray, declare God's Kingdom). This section of scripture begins with Jesus sending the seventy-two "ahead of him to every town and place where he was about to go" (v. 1). The passage ends with His instruction to tell the people that "the kingdom of God is near you" (v. 9). In a similar manner, Isaiah 62:11 states that the Lord's proclamation goes out to the ends of the earth: "Say to the Daughter of Zion, 'See, your Savior comes!'"

There is a sense in which this declaration of the advancement of the Kingdom of God is prophetic: By proclaiming that the Kingdom of God is coming near, we literally "call into being that which is not" (see Romans 4:17). In other words, we are not only declaring our desired state of affairs, but also inviting God to send His heavenly host into our midst.

In summary, the Highway of Holiness concept in Isaiah 62:10–12 elaborates upon and extends the model of Prayer Evangelism by adding a geographical dimension to it. It builds upon the models of evangelism popularized by men such as David Brainerd, George Whitefield, and Francis Asbury, but it also represents a "paradigm shift" from these earlier models. When zealous missionaries and evangelists applied the models from the Great Awakenings in the past, they often directed a spirit of criticism toward those who refused to follow their methods. Instead of winning them over to Christ, and seeing the Kingdom of God advance in their midst, they created an atmosphere of suspicion, distrust, and hatred in many established churches. And as the result of this criticism, "threatening clouds" came over entire denominations and geographic regions, clouds that eventually choked off every wave of national revival that came to the United States.

For this reason, we must go back to the ancient "wells of revival" and prayerfully determine how these reservoirs of spiritual life became clogged. Isaiah 62:10–12 provides a strategy to help unclog them by preparing the way for the Lord to revisit these wells and to open new wells of revival in the 21st century.

———

A Case Study:
Highways of Holiness in New York (1858)

William C. Conant was an eyewitness to the Third Great Awakening, which spread from New York City throughout the world. His 1858 book, **Narratives of Remarkable Conversions and Revival Incidents,** provides fascinating accounts of how this revival spread from city to city. To illustrate how the concept of Highways of Holiness applied in that great move of God, we quote at length from his book.

THE GREAT AWAKENING OF 1857–'8

On the 14th of October, 1857, the financial disorder which had prevailed with increasing severity for many weeks, reached its crisis in an overwhelming panic that prostrated the whole monetary system of the country, virtually in one hour. The struggle was over. . . .

Among the beginning of the Revival in this City [New York] is to be mentioned the enterprise of "Systematic Visitation." Some time ago, a plan was set on foot, which was adopted by a large number of churches, of various denominations, in this city and

Brooklyn, for the purpose of promoting attendance at divine service on the Sabbath, by systematic visitation of assigned neighborhoods. Each church that entered into the enterprise was allotted a certain bound, or parish, of which it was the center, in which every house was to be visited and the religious condition of every family inquired into. The districts at first chosen to be visited were chiefly poor and low neighborhoods, where both the temporal and spiritual destitution of the people were painfully apparent. Parents were solicited to go either to the church in the district, or to some other out of it which they might prefer instead, and to send their children to the Sunday, the Mission, or the Industrial School. In this way thousands of persons, many of whom were formerly degraded and vicious, have been reclaimed to a better moral character and a higher social standing. **Gradually this scheme of visitation was extended so as to include the respectable and fashionable streets, as well as the "highways and hedges," until finally no "passover" was written even on a brown-stone front, and Fifth avenue itself was not left to be exempt.** *And from the reports that have been presented, the results of these efforts, as seen among the higher classes of society, have been of equal interest with those in the lower. The number of rich people, who were never found to attend any church, was enormous. Another of the antecedents of the revival, has been an increased activity in the Sunday Schools. Many of the Sunday Schools, particularly of this city, have, within a very recent period, doubled, and in some instances, tripled their membership; and many conversions have occurred among the young people who attend them as scholars. Many new Mission Sunday Schools have been established in various parts of the city, sustained by individual churches in the neighborhood.*[8] [emphasis added]

Conant then gives page after page of accounts of how the revival spread from Manhattan to Brooklyn (which was a separate city from

New York at that time) and across the United States. We end this section by describing how the revival spread across the Hudson River to New Jersey.

> *Rev. Dr. Scott of Newark, states that the conversion of persons of the strongest and maturest mind in the community, is among the characteristics of the work of grace in Newark. If he had attempted to select from his congregation forty-five of its strongest minds, he would have generally taken the forty-five who had united with his church by profession.*
>
> *At Paterson, N.J., a Union prayer meeting is held daily between four and five in the afternoon, and in some of the churches extra meetings every evening.*
>
> *In Plainfield, Union prayer meetings are held daily.*
>
> *In Hoboken, the Union prayer meetings at the Town Hall are largely attended, and all the churches are receiving accessions in their membership. The Presbyterian and the Baptist churches in West Hoboken, have both held meetings every evening this month.*
>
> *In Jersey City, nearly all the churches have evening meetings, and large numbers have already professed conversion. A Union prayer meeting is held at the Lyceum, in Grand Street, every morning, between the hours of seven and nine, which are animated and interesting. A prayer meeting is also held at the rooms of the Young Men's Christian Association, from half-past five to half-past six o'clock every afternoon.*[9]

This case study provides evidence that Highways of Holiness help prepare the way for the Lord by eliminating geographical barriers that divide the Body of Christ. When the spiritual climate changes in one geographical area, a Highway of Holiness can become a route that God uses to awaken the Body of Christ in other areas. By this method, clouds of darkness can be removed from entire regions or nations. Isaiah 66:8 suggests that a country can be born in a day, and a nation brought forth in a moment. Then all things will be made new, and all that was lost in the Fall of Man will be restored. We will consider these issues in the final two chapters of this book.

PRAYER

O Lord, give me a clear vision about my Highway of Holiness. Grant me the desire and the ability to prepare the way for the people, to build up the highway, and to restore the places that are in ruins. Allow me to see my Highway of Holiness not as it is in the natural, but as you envision it to be when Jesus will come to claim His holy and spotless bride. Give me boldness to proclaim your glory to the nations and to prepare men and women for the triumphant return of the Sun of Righteousness. Amen.

CHAPTER NINE

The Clouds Will be Rolled Back

The happy period in which we live, and the times of refreshing from the presence of the Lord, wherewith you were visited in Northampton . . . often brings to mind that prophecy, Isaiah 59:19: "So shall they fear the name of the Lord from the west, and revere his glory from the rising of the sun. When the enemy shall come in as a flood, the Spirit of the Lord shall lift up a standard against him." I cannot help thinking that this prophecy eminently points at our times; and begins to be fulfilled in the multitudes of souls that are bringing in to fear the Lord, to worship God in Christ, in whom his name is, and to see his glory in his sanctuary. And it is, to me, pretty remarkable, that the prophet here foretells that they should do so, in the period he points at, not from east to west, but from west to east; mentioning the west before the east, contrary to the usual way of speaking in other prophecies, as where Malachi foretells, that the name of the Lord shall be great among the Gentiles, from the rising of the sun to the west (Malachi 1:11) and our Lord Jesus, that many should come from the east and the west &c. (Matthew 8:11). **But the prophet here, under the conduct of the Holy Spirit, who chooses all his words in infinite wisdom, puts the west before the east; intend-**

153

*ing, as I conceive, thereby to signify, that the glorious revival of religion, and the wide and diffuse spread of vital Christianity, in the latter times of the gospel, should begin in the more **westerly** parts, and proceed to these more **easterly**. . . .*
—*Letter from Rev. William McCullough of Scotland to Jonathan Edwards in 1743* [emphasis added]

Rev. William McCullough was one of Scotland's outstanding evangelical pastors during the 18th century. During his ministry there was a great Presbyterian revival at Cambalusing in 1742–44, in which crowds of up to 50,000 attended mass evangelistic campaigns. McCullough began reading accounts about the Edwards and Whitefield revivals that began in New England in 1739, and he prepared the hearts of his congregation by offering an entire year of sermons on regeneration (in 1742) and by conducting concerts of prayer for the revival of religion. He knew that the hope for revival in Cambalusing had come in from the west through the campaigns and writings of Jonathan Edwards, George Whitefield, and other revival leaders in America.

When the "threatening clouds" came over New England in 1743 and began to quench the First Great Awakening, Edwards wrote a note to McCullough, explaining the situation to him and asking him to pray for a new wave of revival in New England. McCullough replied to Edwards in August that year, as described in the passage given above. His studies of the Bible led him to believe that the "threatening clouds" noted by Edwards would be pushed back one day, starting from the west and moving to the east. He comforted Edwards by stating that

God will revive his work again, ere long, and that it will not wholly cease, till it has subdued the whole earth; and, without pretending to prophecy, to hint a little at the ground of my expec-

tations. Only I'm afraid (which is a thing you do not hint at) that before these glorious times, some dreadful stroke or trial may yet be abiding us. May the Lord prepare us for it. But as to this, I cannot and dare not peremptorily determine. All things I give up to further light, without pretending to fix the times and seasons for God's great and wonderful works, which he has reserved in his own power, and the certain knowledge of which he has locked up in his own breast. [1]

Let us consider the following three questions:

➢ **Question One: What must happen before these clouds are rolled back?**

➢ **Question Two: Why did McCullough and Edwards have the sense that one day these clouds would be rolled back from the west to the east?**

➢ **Question Three: How should we pray to God for revival, so that these things might happen in our lifetime rather than in a future generation?**

What Must Happen Before These Clouds are Rolled Back?

Edwards noted that excessive enthusiasm, spirits of contention and jealousy, and a judgmental attitude toward unsaved clergy had divided the church in New England in 1742 and the first half of 1743. We reviewed these issues in Chapter Five and do not need to say more about them in this chapter. The Isaiah 59:19 passage quoted above by McCullough tells us that three events must happen before these dark clouds are removed:

- They shall fear the name of the Lord from the west.
- They shall revere His glory from the rising of the sun.

- The Spirit of the Lord shall lift up a standard against the enemy.

To better understand the meaning of these three events, let us turn to the second of our three questions.

Why Must They be Rolled Back from West to East?

In Chapter Two we noted that seven spirits of God are mentioned in Revelation 1:4 and that these are linked to the seven eyes of Jesus Christ in Revelation 5:6. We then related the idea of seven spirits of God to the seven spirits mentioned in Isaiah 11:2 and noted the following grouping of spirits:

- The Spirit of the Lord appears first and by itself.
- The Spirit of Wisdom and the Spirit of Understanding are paired.
- The Spirit of Counsel and the Spirit of Power are paired.
- The Spirit of Knowledge and the Spirit of the Fear of the Lord are paired.

A key to understanding these passages is the word *spirit,* which is the Greek word *pneuma.* While *pneuma* can refer to a "spirit" in the heavenly realms, it also means "wind." Bearing this in mind, let's look at four different types of winds that are mentioned in the Old Testament.[2]

1. The North Wind

In scripture the north wind represents the fragrant presence of God. In Song of Songs 4:16, for example, we read, "Awake, north wind, and come, south wind! Blow on my garden, that its fragrance may spread abroad. Let my lover come into his garden and taste its choice fruits." In similar manner, Proverbs 25:23 tells us that "a north wind brings rain," which is another sign of the presence of God. And Ezekiel 1:4 (NKJV) says, "Then I looked, and behold, a whirlwind was coming out of the north." This whirlwind is clearly a reference to the presence of God, coming from the north.

2. The South Wind

In scripture the south wind brings provision. In Psalm 78:26–27 (NKJV), for example, we read, "He caused an east wind to blow in the heavens; and by His power he brought in the south wind. He also rained meat on them like the dust, feathered fowl like the sand of the seas." The supply of meat and fowl came via a south wind. From Zechariah 9:11–14 (NKJV) we read in verse 14, "The Lord GOD will blow the trumpet, and go with whirlwinds from the south." In this passage the south wind will restore Ephraim and Zion with a double portion of provision. And, as noted above, Song of Songs 4:16 states that "choice fruits" will come in by means of a south wind.

3. The East Wind

In scripture the east wind signifies judgment, power, and might. We see, for example, that an east wind supplied power and might to divide the Red Sea in Exodus 14:21. In Genesis 41:5–7 an east wind brought blight to the grain fields of Egypt in Pharaoh's dream. In Exodus 10:12–13 an east wind brought a plague of locusts to Egypt. And in Isaiah 41:2 a helper of Israel stirs up an east wind, "calling him in righteousness to his service."

4. The West Wind

In scripture the west wind brings deliverance. In Exodus 10:19 we read, "And the LORD changed the wind to a very strong west wind, which caught up the locusts and carried them into the Red Sea. Not a locust was left anywhere in Egypt." This is no ordinary breeze, which can remove the locusts for a limited time, but rather an extraordinary, supernatural kind of breeze that completely delivered Egypt from the plague of locusts.

We can summarize these four types of winds in the following table.

Table 2: The Four Winds in the Bible

Type of Wind	Scripture Verses	Significance
North Wind	Song of Songs 4:16 Proverbs 25:23 Ezekiel 1:4	The presence of God
South Wind	Psalm 78:26–27 Zechariah 9:14 Song of Songs 4:16	Provision
East Wind	Exodus 14:21 Genesis 41:5–7 Exodus 10:12–13 Isaiah 41:2	Judgment, Power, and Might
West Wind	Exodus 10:19	Deliverance

Now, let's relate these four winds to the seven spirits listed in Isaiah 11:2:

Table 3: The Seven Spirits and the Four Winds

Spirits in Isaiah 11:2	Type of Wind	Significance
The Spirit of the LORD will rest on him	North Wind	The presence of God
The Spirit of wisdom and of understanding	South Wind	Provision
The Spirit of counsel and of power	East Wind	Judgment, Power, and Might
The Spirit of knowledge and of the fear of the LORD	West Wind	Deliverance

Table 3 demonstrates that the four sections of Isaiah 11:2 may be grouped based on the four types of winds:

- The North Wind, which represents the Spirit of the Lord,
- The South Wind, which represents wisdom and under-standing,
- The East Wind, which represents counsel and power (or might), and

- The West Wind, which represents knowledge and fear of the Lord.

This interpretation not only ties together Isaiah 11:2 with the references to the seven spirits in Revelation, but also helps us understand the spiritual operations associated with each of the four types of wind referred to in the Old Testament scriptures.

With this background, we are now able to answer Question Two. The clouds that came over the Thirteen Colonies during the First Great Awakening must be pushed back by a *west wind* in order to deliver this nation from the residual effects of 18th century controversies. As we suggested in Chapter Five, during the First Great Awakening considerable damage was done to the Body

> **The clouds that came over the Thirteen Colonies during the First Great Awakening must be pushed back by a *west wind* in order to deliver this nation from the residual effects of 18th century controversies.**

of Christ through excessive enthusiasm, contention, jealousy, and a judgmental attitude toward unconverted clergy. In their zeal to see men and women born again in Christ (John 3:3), the 18th century revivalists overlooked Jesus' command not to judge others (Matthew 7:1), as well as His instructions on how Christian workers are to go out into the harvest field (Luke 10:1–9).

I believe that this is the reason why Isaiah 59:19 tells us,

From the west, men will fear the name of the LORD, and from the rising of the sun, they will revere his glory. For he will come like a pent-up flood that the breath of the LORD drives along.

The **west wind** must come in to deliver the land and the people from past bondages. And then, after this deliverance has occurred, the **east wind** will usher in the glory, power, and majesty of the Lord, who will return to claim the church as His bride.

How Should We Pray for Revival?

Finally, the answer to Question Three follows directly from Table 3. Given that Isaiah 59:19 tells us the clouds will be moved back from west to east, the spiritual operations that are first needed are Knowledge and Fear of the Lord—the same ones we identified in Chapters Four and Five. As in the days of Brainerd and White-field, the U.S. church today needs an awakening based on these two spiritual operations—plus the principles of Prayer Evangelism Jesus described in Luke 10. *Once these keys to spiritual awakening are understood by pastors, teachers, intercessors, and market-place leaders, we will be able to develop effective strategies to transform our churches, cities, and entire nations for Jesus*

Christ. These strategies, in turn, will lead us into agreement with Jonathan Edwards' prayer for a greater, longer-lasting spiritual awakening:

> *Many high professors [of religion] are fallen, some into gross im-*
> *moralities, some into a rooted spiritual pride, enthusiasm, and an*
> *incorrigible wildness of behaviour, some into a cold frame of mind,*
> *showing a great indifference to the things of religion. But there are*
> *many, and I hope those the greater part of those that were pro-*
> *fessed converts, who appear hitherto like the good ground, and*
> *notwithstanding the thick and dark clouds that so soon follow that*
> *blessed sunshine that we have had; yet I cannot but steadfastly*
> *maintain a hope and a persuasion that God will revive his work,*
> *and that what has been so great and very extraordinary, is a fore-*
> *runner of a yet more glorious and extensive work.*[3]

When the Sun of Righteousness (Malachi 4:2) returns to earth, we will see the ultimate revival:

> *"[T]he dwelling of God is with men, and he will live with them.*
> *They will be his people, and God himself will be with them and be*
> *their God. He will wipe every tear from their eyes. There will be no*
> *more death or mourning or crying or pain, for the old order of*
> *things has passed away."* —Revelation 21:3–4

In the final chapter we will consider how Highways of Holiness can help us to prepare the way for this great restoration of all that was lost.

PRAYER

Father, we believe that you desire to push back the clouds of darkness that are presently over this region. We have experienced foretastes of heaven and have heard wondrous accounts of past spiritual awakenings in this area and in other parts of the world. O Father, we beseech you to send your winds of revival to us in this generation. As we look toward the west, teach us to have a godly fear of the name of the Lord. And as we extend our gaze toward the east, allow us to see the glory of the Sun of Righteousness returning to this place in judgment, power, and might. Send the Spirit of the Lord to us as a standard that will remove the dark and threatening clouds that have kept your church from being that spotless bride of Christ that you desire it to be. In Jesus' name we pray. Amen.

CHAPTER TEN

Restoring All That Was Lost

In the morning was fair weather, and our master sent John Col-
man, with four other men in our boat over to the north side to
sound the other river, being four leagues from us. . . . The land
they told us was as pleasant with grass and flowers, and goodly
trees, as ever they had seen, and very sweet smells came from them.
—Robert Juet's Journal of the Half Moon *landing in the New*
York Harbor on September 6, 1609[1]

How the Land Became Defiled

Historical accounts by the Dutch and English tell us that the
Hudson River Valley was an exceptionally beautiful place during the
17th century. Henry Hudson and his crew members remarked on
the land's beauty when they landed at the New York harbor in
September of 1609. In their prize-winning book, **Gotham,** Edwin
Burrows and Mike Wallace write about the amazing diversity of
wildlife that lived in the Hudson Valley at that time:

> *But it was the miraculous size and quantity and variety of*
> *things—the sheer prodigality of life—that left the most lasting*
> *impression. Travelers spoke of vast meadows of grass "as high as a*
> *man's middle" and forests with towering stands of walnut, cedar,*

chestnut, maple, and oak. Orchards bore apples of incomparable sweetness and "pears larger than a fist." Every spring the hills and fields were dyed red with ripening strawberries, and so many birds filled the woods "that men can scarcely go through them for the whistling, the noise, and the chattering." Boats crossing the bay were escorted by schools of playful whales, seals, and porpoises. Twelve-inch oysters and six-foot lobsters crowded offshore waters, and so many fish thrived in streams and ponds that they could be taken by hand. Woods and tidal marshlands teemed with bears, wolves, foxes, raccoons, otters, beavers, quail, partridge, forty-pound wild turkeys, doves "so numerous that the light can hardly be discerned when they fly," and countless deer "feeding, or gamboling or resting in the shades in full view." Wild swans were so plentiful "that the bays and shores where they resort appear as if they were dressed in white drapery." Blackbirds roosted together in such numbers that one hunter killed 170 with a single shot; another bagged eleven sixteen-pound gray geese the same way.[2]

Artist's sketch of Henry Hudson's **Half Moon**[3]

To the early Dutch settlers in New York and New Jersey, this region was a veritable paradise. The Lenape Indians who inhabited the area were wary of the strange boats and white men who accompanied Henry Hudson on the 1609 voyage, but their curiosity soon led to bartering for imported goods. The Dutch visitors offered such articles as knives, guns, and kitchenware in exchange for food, clothing, furs, and other items from the Indians.

Although the Lenapes remained suspicious of the Dutch, they allowed them to settle in New Amsterdam and across the river at what is today Jersey City, New Jersey. Relationships between the Dutch and the Lenapes were originally cordial, as evidenced by several exchanges of land for European imports (most notably, Peter Minuit's purchase of Manhattan Island for twenty-four dollars worth of goods[4]).

As the 17th century progressed, however, these relationships deteriorated badly. In 1639 Dutch Governor William Kieft demanded that the Lenapes living in Manhattan pay "contributions" of wampum, maize, and pelts under the pretense that the Dutch were providing them protection from other hostile Indian tribes. The Lenapes protested this action and grumbled that Kieft "must be a very mean man."[5] Then Kieft ordered an attack on Indians living in Jersey City on a cold night in February 1643. The Dutch soldiers ruthlessly murdered more than eighty Lenape Indians, including women and infants. This massacre led to a reprisal by the twenty Indian tribes living in the Hudson Valley, who proceeded to kill all the Europeans living in Jersey City and burn down their homes. Fear of murder and robberies led the Dutch government to order that all Dutch settlers move into New Amsterdam or into protected communities on the New Jersey side of the Hudson River.[6] In short, the arrogant behavior of the Dutch settlers not only poisoned relationships with the First Nations people but also defiled the land through broken covenants and bloodshed.

Similar defilements of the land occurred at Newark, which lies west of Jersey City along the Passaic River. Puritans from Connecticut purchased the land from the Hackensack Indians in 1667. Most of present-day Essex County was received from the Indians for approximately seven hundred dollars.[7] Newark was established as the last Puritan theocracy in the Thirteen Colonies and maintained relatively harmonious relationships with the Indians during its early history. But a series of land disputes between Newark and the British proprietors of East Jersey (as it was then called) led to subsequent controversies between Newark and Elizabeth that lasted until after the Revolutionary War.

> **Our only hope is for a great Christ-awakening, which will fulfill the promise of Luke 19:10: ". . . to seek and to save *that which was lost."***

In the 1750s and 1760s the first highways in the Colonies were built to promote commerce. While these highways helped to generate economic and population growth in Newark, they also caused dramatic increases in crime in Essex and surrounding counties. To combat the problem of law-breaking caused by tramps coming in from New York and Philadelphia, Newark passed a law declaring that horse thievery was a crime punishable by death. Puritan moral values declined steadily during the 18th century, and after the Revolutionary War the Body of Christ was split for more than one hundred years over a dispute about harvesting of wheat on the Sabbath.[8] Thus, while Newark began as a godly city and kept good relations with the First Nations peoples, the land became defiled through broken covenants, violence, and disunity within the Protestant churches. These defilements were never addressed as spiritual issues, which undoubtedly contributed to Newark's economic and spiritual decline during the 19th and 20th centuries.

This brief spiritual history of New York and Northern New Jersey traces some of the basic issues that caused defilement of the land. Over the centuries this region has changed dramatically due to population growth and heavy urban development, but the spiritual climate has also changed dramatically. As the result of the defilements noted above, the following shifts have occurred:

- Man's relationship to the *land* has changed. Many species of wildlife that were present in 1609 have left the region or were killed off by European settlers.
- Man's relationship to the *marketplace* has been impacted. Pressures for development have produced a steady decline in agriculture in the "Garden State," and most people in this region now work in the service or manufacturing sectors. This region is now one of the most expensive metropolitan areas in the U.S.
- *Social relationships* have been greatly impacted. Newark, Jersey City, and surrounding cities experienced serious race riots during the 1960s, and the crime rate has remained high since that time. Large areas of these cities are no longer safe places to live or work.
- Northern New Jersey and New York are becoming increasingly secularized compared to previous generations. A growing number of people are *spiritually* alienated from their Creator.

The changes in these four areas—the land, the marketplace, social relationships, and spirituality—are reflections of what happened to the human race in the Garden of Eden. Through the fall of Adam and Eve, the entire race became alienated from the land, the marketplace, other human beings, and God. Only the death and resurrection of Jesus Christ can reverse these situations. Our only hope is for a great Christ-awakening,[9] which will fulfill the promise of Luke 19:10: "For the Son of Man has come to seek and to save *that which was lost*" (NASB, emphasis added). This last phrase, "that which was lost," refers not only to spiritual brokenness, but also to man's relationships with the land, the marketplace, and society.[10]

Why the Land Must be Healed

When God decides to restore a city or nation, He often begins by healing the land.[11] In Ezekiel 36, for example, God began the restoration of Israel by instructing Ezekiel to speak directly to the **land:**

> *"Therefore prophesy concerning the land of Israel and say to the mountains and hills, to the ravines and valleys: 'This is what the Sovereign LORD says: I speak in my jealous wrath because you have suffered the scorn of the nations. Therefore this is what the Sovereign LORD says: I swear with uplifted hand that the nations around you will also suffer scorn. But you, O mountains of Israel, will produce branches and fruit for my people Israel, for they will soon come home.'"* —Ezekiel 36:6–8

After the land was restored, God then told Ezekiel to speak to the **dry bones** (the people of Israel who had died):

> *Then he said to me, "Prophesy to these bones and say to them, 'Dry bones, hear the word of the LORD! This is what the Sovereign LORD says to these bones: I will make breath enter you, and you will come to life.'"* —Ezekiel 37:4–5

This pattern is parallel to the creation of the world as described in Genesis 1. God created the land, sea, vegetation, and all kinds of living creatures before He created Adam and Eve, so humans would have dominion over every other living creature. God understands that His people cannot prosper if the land is unfruitful and defiled.

For this reason He makes His people responsible for stewardship of both the land as well as the creatures inhabiting the earth.

In the Bible God tells us there are at least four major categories of things that defile the land: idolatry, immorality, bloodshed, and broken covenants. Let's review each of these causes of defilement briefly, using Alistair Petrie's book ***Releasing Heaven on Earth***[12] as a guide:

1. Idolatry

"Idolatry is the most serious sin in the eyes of God. We commit it when we allow anyone or anything else to take priority in our lives over Him. It is always connected with worship and involves honoring a spirit form other than God."

2. Sexual Immorality

"Idolaters are often led into immoral lifestyles because they have no sense of accountability before a living God. Leviticus 18:1–23 gives extensive insight into the issue of sexual impropriety. . . . Notice again that our territory of influence and authority as God's people are reduced when we do not address prostitution in a forthright manner. . . . When the church does not address immorality and fornication, she loses her 'authority' in that location."

3. Bloodshed

"Bloodshed includes the taking of innocent life and the untimely slaughter of suppressed people groups. Bloodshed of any type, from the past or in the present, affects us in a variety of ways, and often results in the nursing of criticism, anger, jealousy, bitterness and rage over succeeding generations."

4. Broken Covenants

"Isaiah 24:5–6 states that 'the earth is defiled by its people; they have disobeyed the laws, violated the statutes and broken the everlasting covenant. Therefore a curse consumes the earth; its people must bear that guilt.' . . . In the New Testament God renews His covenant with the human race through Jesus Christ, and, as with

all covenants, seals it in blood. . . . This is divine love at its best! But when a person or the Church violates that covenant, we make ourselves vulnerable to the consequences of broken promises at personal, family, church, community, city and even national levels."

These four biblical sources of defilement are summarized below in Table 4.

Table 4: Four Things that Defile the Land

Type of Defilement	Scripture Verses	Significance
Idolatry	Jeremiah 3:6–10 Jeremiah 16:18	God will repay double for defiling the land with idols.
Sexual Immorality	Leviticus 18:22 Leviticus 19:29 Jeremiah 3:1–2, 9 Ezekiel 16:25–27	Sexual immorality reduces the influence and authority of the church and can increase the individual's personal lust for authority and power.
Bloodshed	Numbers 35:33–34 Isaiah 59:1–3	Bloodshed pollutes and defiles the land.
Broken Covenants	Isaiah 24:5–6	A curse consumes the earth because the people have broken God's laws, statutes, and covenants.

Source: Alistair Petrie[13]

Once the land has been cleansed from these four sources of defilement, God will bless His people and make them fruitful and good stewards of the land. Petrie notes that there is an integral connection between the condition of the land and the condition of the people:

> *Scripture makes it quite clear that good roots will always yield good fruit. As God's stewards of the land, we have been given His authority to remove all unholy roots and foundations that were never part of His plan and purpose for us. At the same time, we can add new foundations to the holy ones that already exist. Together, these foundations of our lives are to bring Him honour and glory, and will release and reveal His redemptive purposes for His people and for His land.*[14]

The Highways of Holiness Strategy

In February 2000 Graham Power, a South African businessman, received the first of a series of visions about how God was planning to reach the entire African continent for Jesus Christ. Power understood that God wanted to build one spiritual highway across Africa, from Cape Town to Cairo (south to north) and another one from Senegal to Somalia (west to east). Power saw that as these spiritual highways intersected, they would superimpose a cross over the whole continent of Africa.

That year he and his colleagues established Transformation Africa as an organization to bring renewal to entire nations. What began in 2001 as a canopy of prayer over Cape Town, South Africa, became a continent-wide movement in 2004. In 2005 Transformation Africa combined with leading prayer groups on six continents to coordinate the first-ever Global Day of Prayer. It is estimated that more than 200 million people around the world participated in this global outpouring of the Lord's blessing.[15]

Through these Highways of Holiness, the Lord is reaching every nation in Africa and causing a wildfire of evangelism. Even **National Geographic** magazine has noted that something remarkable is happening to transform Africa from a continent of despair to one of renewal.[16]

Power described these visions and a number of scriptures from Isaiah that confirmed the strategy of developing a Highway of Holiness:

- *Isaiah 62:10 — Pass through, pass through the gates! Prepare the way for the people. Build up, build up the highway! Remove the stones. Raise a banner for the nations.*

- *Isaiah 60:18 — "No longer will violence be heard in your land, nor ruin or destruction within your borders, but you will call your walls Salvation and your gates Praise."*

- *Isaiah 60:22 — "The least of you will become a thousand, the smallest a mighty nation. I am the LORD; in its time I will do this swiftly."*

- *Isaiah 65:1–2 — "I revealed myself to those who did not ask for me; I was found by those who did not seek me. To a nation that did not call on my name, I said, 'Here am I, here am I.' All day long I have held out my hands to an obstinate people, who walk in ways not good, pursuing their own imaginations."*

- *Isaiah 66:8 — "Who has ever heard of such a thing? Who has ever seen such things? Can a country be born in a day or a nation be brought forth in a moment?"*

- *Isaiah 61:8 — "For I, the LORD, love justice; I hate robbery and iniquity. In my faithfulness I will reward them and make an everlasting covenant with them."*

- *Isaiah 66:18 — "And I, because of their actions and their imaginations, am about to come and gather all nations and tongues, and they will come and see my glory."*

A Strategy for New Jersey

As I heard Graham Power describe how these verses confirmed the strategy he received for the transformation of Africa,[17] I recognized that these were many of the same verses I had been praying about for my home state of New Jersey. Then I recalled my repeated thoughts about a "Highway of Holiness" during recent months, and wondered: Could it be that the Lord wants to use the same strategy to transform New Jersey that He revealed in Africa? Is He putting new meaning into Isaiah's prophecies about a way of holiness?

I believe He is. Consider the words of the Lord in Isaiah 43:19:

> *"See, I am doing a new thing! Now it springs up; do you not perceive it? I am making a way in the desert and streams in the wasteland."*

Reflecting on these things, I visualized a map of New Jersey, overlaid with the cross of Jesus:

But why, I wondered, would God want to build Highways of Holiness in a region? As I reflected further, I realized that this strategy would produce the following benefits:

- *Highways of Holiness link together Kingdom-minded people who live in different communities.* Isaiah 35:8 tells us that "it will be for those who walk in that Way; wicked fools will not go about on it."
- *Highways of Holiness facilitate the flow of people and materials that are needed to rebuild decayed cities.* Isaiah 61:4 says, "[T]hey will renew the ruined cities that have been devastated for generations."
- *Highways of Holiness infuse hope into situations that appear hopeless from a human perspective.* Isaiah 61:7 tells us, "Instead of their shame my people will receive a double portion, and instead of disgrace they will rejoice in their inheritance; and so they will inherit a double portion in their land, and everlasting joy will be theirs."
- *Highways of Holiness enable the people of God to take back land that has been stolen by the enemy.* When Jesus sent out the seventy-two disciples in Luke 10, they returned with joy and said, "Lord, even the demons submit to us in your name" (Luke 10:17).
- *Highways of Holiness change the spiritual climate by inviting the Kingdom of God into the present situation.* In Luke 10:9, Jesus tells the seventy-two, "Heal the sick who are there and tell them, 'The Kingdom of God is near you.'"
- *Finally, Highways of Holiness help to prepare the way for Jesus' return to earth.* In Isaiah 62:11 the prophet writes, "The LORD has made proclamation to the ends of the earth: 'Say to the Daughter of Zion, "See, your Savior comes!"'"

What an exciting time this is for the Body of Christ! Just as God used circuit riders to spread the gospel quickly from community to community during the 19th century,[18] today He wants to use 21st century circuit riders to prepare for Jesus' return to earth as its triumphant King. And even now He is knocking at our door, inviting us to join in the rebuilding of cities and the ingathering of lost souls. Perhaps—even at this moment—He is using this message to speak to you about building your own Highway of Holiness.

> **In the present day an increasing number of Christians are being called to go from city to city, to share the Good News and to seek and to save all that was lost in the Fall.**

Going from City to City

The prophet Zechariah tells us that God's people will travel from one city to another, inviting others to seek the Lord. In chapter 8, verses 20–21, Zechariah writes,

> *This is what the LORD Almighty says: "Many peoples and the inhabitants of many cities will yet come, and the inhabitants of one city will go to another and say, 'Let us go at once to entreat the LORD and seek the LORD Almighty. I myself am going.'"*

In the present day an increasing number of Christians are being called to go from city to city, raising up pastors, intercessors, government officials, educators, worship leaders, youth leaders, and businesspeople wherever they go. Intercessors from one city are traveling to other cities along a Highway of Holiness to share the Good News and to seek and to save all that was lost in the Fall. In New Jersey, for instance, as intercessors go up and down this highway, some are reporting that the heavens are beginning to open over the Garden State.

The Bible gives three specific references to the concept of "open heavens": Genesis 28:10–22 (Jacob's dream about the stairway to heaven), Malachi 3:10 (how tithing will open the floodgates of heaven), and John 1:51 (where Nathaniel is promised that he will see heaven open). The common theme in these passages is how God honors His eternal covenants. At Bethel, for example, God reminded Jacob that

> *"I am the LORD, the God of your father Abraham and the God of Isaac. I will give you and your descendants the land on which you are lying. Your descendants will be like the dust of the earth, and you will spread out to the west and to the east, to the north and to the south. All peoples on earth will be blessed through you and your offspring. I am with you and will watch over you wherever you go, and I will bring you back to this land. I will not leave you until I have done what I have promised you."—Genesis 28:13–15*

At Divident Hill and other places, intercessors are reporting occurrences of an open heaven as they pray to renew age-old covenants in New Jersey. As they travel from city to city and come into agreement with the prayers of past generations, the Lord is revealing more and more of His presence in this region.

In similar fashion elsewhere in the United States and many other nations, the prayer movement is taking back ground from the enemy as believers travel along Highways of Holiness, praising the Lord and announcing that the Kingdom of God is at hand. America's godly heritage is without a doubt its greatest resource. Throughout its history, Christians have consecrated their homes, businesses, and cities by making godly covenants. These covenants, like the prayers of the saints described in Revelation 5:8, are being stored up in bowls in heaven.

As church and marketplace leaders come to recognize the principles we have discussed in this book—stones of remembrance, wells of revival, healing the land, and Highways of Holiness—they will be well equipped to develop effective strategies to transform churches, cities, and entire nations for Jesus Christ. I myself am traveling on my Highway of Holiness. Won't you join me by going on yours?

PRAYER

O Lord our God, forgive us and our forefathers for the things we have done that have defiled your land. We repent that our idolatry, immorality, shedding of blood, and broken covenants have polluted the land and have offended your holy name. Give us spiritual discernment to see these defilements as you see them. Grant us wisdom and courage to cleanse the land of these past defilements. And release us with joy as we go from city to city, dedicating Highways of Holiness that prepare the way for the return of Jesus Christ, in all His fullness. Since we are heirs of your eternal covenant to Abraham and Isaac, we believe that you will lead us back to the promised land. We also believe that Jesus Christ will restore all things that were lost at the Fall of Man. We affirm all these things in His mighty name. Amen.

Appendix A:
Scriptures About the
Highway of Holiness

Isaiah 35:8 — And a highway will be there; it will be called the Way of Holiness. The unclean will not journey on it; it will be for those who walk in that Way; wicked fools will not go about on it.

Isaiah 40:3–5 — A voice of one calling: "In the desert prepare the way for the LORD; make straight in the wilderness a highway for our God. Every valley shall be raised up, every mountain and hill made low; the rough ground shall become level, the rugged places a plain. And the glory of the LORD will be revealed, and all mankind together will see it. For the mouth of the LORD has spoken."

Isaiah 57:14–15 — "Build up, build up, prepare the road! Remove the obstacles out of the way of my people." For this is what the high and lofty One says—he who lives forever, whose name is holy: "I live in a high and holy place, but also with him who is contrite and lowly in spirit, to revive the spirit of the lowly and to revive the heart of the contrite."

Isaiah 60:18, 22 — "No longer will violence be heard in your land, nor ruin or destruction within your borders, but you will call your walls Salvation and your gates Praise. . . . The least of you will become a thousand, the smallest a mighty nation."

Isaiah 61:4–9 —— They will rebuild the ancient ruins and restore the places long devastated; they will renew the ruined cities that have been devastated for generations. Aliens will shepherd your flocks; foreigners will work your fields and vineyards. And you will be called priests of the LORD, you will be named ministers of our God. You will feed on the wealth of nations, and in their riches you will boast. Instead of their shame my people will receive a double portion, and instead of disgrace they will rejoice in their inheritance; and so they will inherit a double portion in their land, and everlasting joy will be theirs. "For I, the LORD, love justice; I hate robbery and iniquity. In my faithfulness I will reward them and make an everlasting covenant with them. Their descendants will be known among the nations and their offspring among the peoples. All who see them will acknowledge that they are a people the LORD has blessed."

Isaiah 62:10–12 —— Pass through, pass through the gates! Prepare the way for the people. Build up, build up the highway! Remove the stones. Raise a banner for the nations. The LORD has made proclamation to the ends of the earth: "Say to the Daughter of Zion, 'See, your Savior comes! See, his reward is with him, and his recompense accompanies him.'" They will be called the Holy People, the Redeemed of the LORD; and you will be called Sought After, the City No Longer Deserted.

Isaiah 66:8 —— "Who has ever heard of such a thing? Who has ever seen such things? Can a country be born in a day or a nation be brought forth in a moment?"

Isaiah 66:18 —— "And I, because of their actions and their imaginations, am about to come and gather all nations and tongues, and they will come and see my glory."

Appendix B:
"Divident Hill" by Mrs. E. C. Kinney

Pause here, O Muse! That Fancy's eye may trace the footprints still,
Of men that, centuries gone by, with prayer ordained this hill;
As lifts the misty veil of years, such visions here arise
As when the glorious past appears before enchanted eyes.

I see, from midst the faithful few whose deeds yet live sublime—
Whose guileless spirits, brave as true, are models "for all time,"
A group upon this height convened—in solemn prayer they stand—
Men on whose sturdy wisdom leaned the settlers of the land.

In mutual love the line they trace that will their houses divide,
And ever mark the chosen place that prayer hath sanctified;
And here it stands—a temple old, which crumbling Time still braves;
Though ages have their cycles rolled above those patriots' graves.

As Christ transfigured on the height the three beheld with awe,
And near his radiant form, in white, the ancient prophets saw;
So, on this summit I behold with beatific sight,
Once more our praying sires of old, as spirits clothed in light.
A halo crowns the sacred hill, and thence glad voices raise
A song that doth the conclave fill—their prayers are turned to praise!
Art may not for these saints of old the marble urn invent;
*Yet here the Future shall behold the Heaven-built monument.**

---

*From Joseph Atkinson, **The History of Newark, New Jersey**
(Newark, N.J.: William B. Guild, 1878), p. 35.

Rededication of Divident Hill in June 2004.
"And every time you do this, . . . you're going to feel His
presence coming in."*

**See page 140.*

Appendix C:
Jonathan Edwards'
Observations on Revival

Jonathan Edwards is widely regarded as America's "theologian of revival." He was not only a brilliant theologian but also an astute observer of contemporary events. Although some people may have the impression that he was detached from the world around him, this was definitely not the case. To the contrary, he voraciously read the American and European newspapers to gain "hopeful signs" of the advancement of the Kingdom of God on both sides of the Atlantic. In addition he was a diligent observer of the mighty work God was doing during the First Great Awakening.

This appendix is included to help you understand how God was at work in New England between 1735 and 1743. Four of Edwards' detailed writings on the subject of revival are provided, which illustrate the astonishing extent to which the presence of God changed the spiritual climate throughout the region. If these quotations whet your appetite to learn more about Jonathan Edwards, good places to start would be his *Memoirs* and *Thoughts on the Revival.* Both of these books are in the public domain and are also included in *The Works of Jonathan Edwards* (Peabody, Mass: Hendrickson Publications, 2004; originally published in 1834).

1. *The year 1735 opened on Northampton in a most auspicious manner. A deep and solemn interest in the great truths of religion, had become universal in all parts of the town, and among all classes of people. This was the only subject of conversation in every company; and almost the only business of the people appeared to be, to secure their salvation. So extensive was the influence of the Spirit of God, that there was scarcely an individual in the town, old or young, who was left unconcerned about the great things of the eternal world. . . . There was scarcely a house which did not furnish the tokens of his presence, and scarcely a family which did not present the trophies of his grace. . . . This was undoubtedly one of the most remarkable events of this kind, that has occurred since the canon of the New Testament was finished. (***Memoirs,*** Chapter VII, p. lxxv)*

2. *And there is the clearest evidence, from what has been observed, that this is the work of God; so it is evident that it is a very great and wonderful and exceedingly glorious work.——This is certain, that it is a great and wonderful event, a strange revolution, an unexpected overturning of things, suddenly brought to pass; such as never has been seen in **New England,** and scarce has been heard of in any land. Who that saw the state of things in **New England** a few years ago, would have thought that in so short a time there would be such a change? (***Thoughts on the Revival,*** Part I, Sect. VI, p. 379)*

3. *I have been particularly acquainted with many persons who have been the subjects of the high and extraordinary transports of the present day. . . . Extraordinary views of divine things, and the religious affections, were frequently attended with very great effects on the body. Nature often sunk under the weight of divine discoveries, and the strength of the body was taken away. The person was deprived of all ability to speak or stand. . . . These effects on the body did not arise from any bodily distemper or weakness, because the greatest of all have been in a good state of health. This quiet*

rejoicing has been with trembling, i.e., attended with a deep and lively sense of the greatness and majesty of God, and the person's own exceeding littleness and vileness. . . . These things already mentioned have been attended also with the following things, viz.: An extraordinary sense of the awful majesty, greatness, and holiness of God, so as sometimes to overwhelm soul and body; a sense of the piercing all-seeing eye of God, so as sometimes to take away the bodily strength; and an extraordinary view of the infinite terribleness of the wrath of God; together with a sense of the ineffable misery of sinners who are exposed to this wrath. . . . A sight of the fullness and glorious sufficiency of Christ, has been so affecting as to overcome the body. (**Thoughts on the Revival,** Part I, Sect. V, pp. 376–77)

4. *Whatever imprudences there have been, and whatever sinful irregularities, . . . yet, it is manifest and notorious, that there has been of late a very uncommon influence upon the minds of a great part of the inhabitants of New England, attended with the best effects. . . . There is a vast increase of concern for the salvation of the precious soul, and of that inquiry, "What shall I do to be saved?" The hearts of multitudes have been greatly taken off from the things of the world, its profits, pleasures, and honours. Multitudes in all parts have had their consciences awakened, and have been made sensible of the pernicious nature and consequences of sin, and what a dreadful thing it is to be under guilt and the displeasure of God, and to live without peace and reconciliation with him.* (**Thoughts on the Revival,** Part I, Sect. IV, p. 374)

Appendix D:
Wells of Revival on Interstate 78

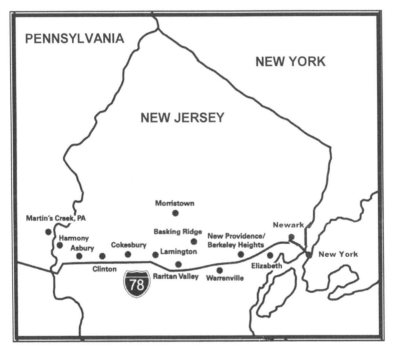

Fourteen Wells of Revival on Interstate 78

1. Martins Creek, PA—Home of David Brainerd during his first ministerial calling to the Delaware Indians (1744)
2. Harmony, NJ—Presbyterian revivals during the 18th and 19th centuries

3. Asbury, NJ—Named for Methodist Bishop Francis Asbury
4. Clinton, NJ—Methodist revival in 1830s
5. Cokesbury, NJ—Named for Methodist Bishop Thomas Coke
6. Lamington, NJ—Lamington Presbyterian Church birthed by Whitefield revival in 1740
7. Raritan Valley, NJ—Dutch Reformed revival under Theodorus Frelinghuysen in 1720s
8. Basking Ridge, NJ—Presbyterian and Methodist revival during Whitefield visit in 1740
9. Morristown, NJ—Methodist revival during Second Great Awakening (1828)
10. Warrenville, NJ—At least seven Baptist revivals during the 19th century at Mt. Bethel Meetinghouse
11. New Providence/Berkeley Heights, NJ—Methodist and Presbyterian revivals in Second Great Awakening
12. Elizabeth, NJ—Numerous Presbyterian and Methodist revivals during the 17th and 18th centuries
13. Newark, NJ—Numerous Presbyterian and Methodist revivals during the 17th and 18th centuries
14. New York City, NY—Businessmen's prayer meetings in 1857–58, which led to a worldwide spiritual awakening

Endnotes

Introduction

1. Joseph Atkinson, *The History of Newark, New Jersey* (Newark, N.J.: William B. Guild, 1878), p. 34.
2. This poem is reprinted in Appendix B.
3. Dutch Sheets and William Ford III, *History Makers* (Ventura, Calif.: Regal Books, 2004), pp. 49–64.
4. Atkinson, *The History of Newark, New Jersey,* p. 33.

Chapter One

1. William Thompson Hanzsche, "The History of Churches in New Jersey," in William Starr Myers, ed., *The Story of New Jersey, Vol. II* (New York: Lewis Historical Publishing Company, n.d.), pp. 299–300.
2. John Greenfield, *Power from on High: The Story of the Great Moravian Revival of 1727* (Bethlehem, Penn.: The Moravian Church in America, 1995). Originally published in 1928.
3. Andrew Jukes, *The Names of God in Holy Scripture* (Grand Rapids, Mich.: Kregel Publications, 1987), pp. 27–28.
4. Note that Knowledge and Fear of the Lord are explicitly linked together in Joshua 4:24. We will expand on this theme in Chapter Two.
5. For a detailed description of national awakenings and their impacts on New Jersey, see my publication, "Wells of Revival in

New Jersey" (2004). This is available from The Caring Network, PO Box 872, New Providence NJ 07974-0872.

6. Dr. Martyn Lloyd-Jones, *Revival* (Wheaton, Ill.: Crossway Books, 1987). This classic book contains twenty-four messages that Lloyd-Jones gave in 1959 to commemorate the Great Revival that spread from New York City to Wales in 1859. See Chapter Seven for further details about this spiritual awakening.

7. George H. Morrison, "The Choked Wells," in Warren W. Wiersbe, ed., *Classic Sermons on Revival and Spiritual Renewal* (Grand Rapids, Mich.: Kregel Publications, 1995). This sermon was originally published in 1904.

8. Lou Engle, *Digging the Wells of Revival* (Shippensburg, Penn.: Destiny Image, 1998).

9. Quoted by Tom Ascol in "Reformation, Revival and the Religious Right," *Founders Journal* 26 (Fall 1996). Available at www.founders.org/FJ26/editorial.html.

Chapter Two

1. Arthur Burk, audiotape series on "The Redemptive Gifts of Individuals" (Whittier, Calif.: Plumbline Ministries, 2000).

2. Todd Bentley, audiotape series on "Encounters of the Throne Room Kind" (Abbotsford, B.C.: Fresh Fire Ministries, 2003).

3. *Thoughts on the Revival,* in *The Works of Jonathan Edwards* (Peabody, Mass.: Hendrickson Publications, 2004) Part I, Sect. V, pp. 376–77; originally published in 1834. *Thoughts on the Revival* was originally published as a separate book in 1743.

4. David W. Kling, *A Field of Divine Wonders: The New Divinity and Village Renewals in Northwestern Connecticut, 1792–1822* (State College, Penn.: The Pennsylvania State University Press, 1993), p. 3.

5. See Bennet Tyler, *New England Revivals as They Existed at the Close of the Eighteenth and the Beginning of the Nine-*

teenth Centuries (Wheaton, Ill.: Richard Owen Roberts Publishers, 1980). These revival accounts were originally published in the *Connecticut Evangelical Magazine* between 1800 and 1803.

6. Nathan Bangs, *A History of the Methodist Episcopal Church* (1853), Volume II, Book IV, Chapter 5.

7. Iain Murray, *Revival and Revivalism: The Making and Marring of Evangelicalism, 1750–1858* (Carlisle, Penn.: Banner of Truth, 1994), p. 148.

8. Jeff Ziegler and Jay Rogers, "Revival and Spiritual Awakening," *The Forerunner,* 1992. Available at www.forerunner.com/forerunner/X0606_Revival__Spiritual_A.html. See also Chapter Seven.

9. The scripture reference for "redigging the wells" is Genesis 26:18. For a recent exposition of this concept, see Lou Engle, *Digging the Wells of Revival* (Shippensburg, Penn.: Destiny Image, 1998). See also Notes 5–8 in Chapter One.

10. John Piper and Justin Taylor, eds., *A God-Entranced Vision of All Things: The Legacy of Jonathan Edwards* (Wheaton, Ill.: Crossway Books, 2004).

11. *A God-Entranced Vision of All Things,* p. 22.

12. Quoted in *A God-Entranced Vision of All Things,* p. 23, emphasis original.

13. J. I. Packer, "The Glory of God and the Reviving of Religion," in Piper and Taylor, *A God-Entranced Vision of All Things,* p. 95.

14. Mark Noll, "Jonathan Edwards, Moral Philosophy, and the Secularization of American Christian Thought," *Reformed Journal* 33 (February 1983), p. 26. Quoted in Piper and Taylor, p. 21.

15. *A God-Entranced Vision of All Things,* p. 14, taken from Edwards' sermon, "The Christian Pilgrim."

16. John Piper, *The Dangerous Duty of Delight: The Glorified God and the Satisfied Soul* (Sisters, Ore.: Multnomah Publishers,

2001), p. 19. Based on Edwards' 1755 book, *The End for Which God Created the World.*

17. George M. Marsden, *Jonathan Edwards: A Life* (New Haven, Conn.: Yale University, 2003), p. 490.

18. *A God-Entranced Vision of All Things,* p. 86.

19. *Memoirs of Jonathan Edwards,* Chapter III, passim; in *The Works of Jonathan Edwards.*

20. Donald Whitney, "Pursuing a Passion for God Through Spiritual Disciplines: Learning from Jonathan Edwards," in Piper and Taylor, *A God-Entranced Vision of All Things,* p. 114.

21. Robert O. Bakke, *The Power of Extraordinary Prayer* (Wheaton, Ill.: Crossway Books, 2000), p. 35.

22. *The Power of Extraordinary Prayer,* p. 59.

23. *The Power of Extraordinary Prayer,* p. 60, originally taken from Edwards' treatise *An Humble Attempt.* Emphasis is Edwards'.

24. *Jonathan Edwards: A Life,* pp. 40–41.

25. *Jonathan Edwards: A Life,* p. 42.

26. *Jonathan Edwards: A Life,* p. 43.

27. Ed Silvoso, *Prayer Evangelism* (Ventura, Calif.: Gospel Light Publications, 2000), p. 35.

28. *Prayer Evangelism,* pp. 37–38.

29. Taken from *Prayer Evangelism,* pp. 37–48.

Chapter Three

1. Peter Wagner and Pablo Deiros, eds., *The Rising Revival: Firsthand Accounts of the Incredible Argentine Revival—and How It Can Spread Throughout the World* (Ventura, Calif.: Gospel Light Publications, 1998).

2. Reverend Pedro Ibarra.

3. For more information about this remarkable healing, see Jane Rumph, *Signs and Wonders in America Today: Amazing*

Accounts of God's Power (Ann Arbor, Mich.: Servant Publications, 2003; now distributed by Regal Books), pp. 62–68.

Chapter Four

1. *The Life and Diary of David Brainerd,* Jonathan Edwards, ed., with a biographical sketch by Philip E. Howard, Jr. (Grand Rapids, Mich.: Baker Book House, 1949), p. 77. Originally published in 1747.

2. This story is from F. W. Boreham's book, *Life Verses: Volume III* (Grand Rapids, Mich.: Kregel Publications, 1994), p. 32. Originally published as *A Casket of Cameos* in 1924 by Epworth Press, London.

3. Eugene Myers Harrison, *Heroes of Faith on Pioneer Trails* (Chicago: Moody Press, 1945).

4. *Life and Diary,* July 21, 1745, p. 208.

5. *Life and Diary,* July 21, 1745, p. 208.

6. *Life and Diary,* p. 247.

7. Crossweeksung was subsequently renamed as Crosswicks. This small, predominantly Quaker community is located about fifteen miles southeast of Trenton.

8. *Life and Diary,* p. 214.

9. *Life and Diary,* p. 214.

10. *Life and Diary,* pp. 215–16.

11. *Life and Diary,* p. 216.

12. *Life and Diary,* pp. 216–18.

13. *Life and Diary,* p. 221.

14. *Life and Diary,* p. 224.

15. *Life and Diary,* pp. 250–51.

16. *Antiquities of the Cherokee Indians.* Compiled from the *Collection of Rev. Daniel Sqabin Buttrick, Their Missionary from 1817 to 1847.* Published at Vinita, Indian Territory, 1884.

17. *Life and Diary,* p. 168.

18. On this point see E. Brooks Holifield, ***Theology in America: Christian Thought from the Age of the Puritans to the Civil War*** (New Haven, Conn.: Yale University Press, 2003), pp. 97–99.

19. ***Life and Diary,*** p. 248.

20. ***Life and Diary,*** p. 170.

21. ***Life and Diary,*** pp. 257–58.

22. ***Life and Diary,*** p. 211.

23. This concept is discussed in greater detail in Chapters Two and Eight. See also Chuck and Nancy Missler, ***Be Ye Transformed*** (Coeur d'Alene, Ida.: The King's High Way Ministries, 1996), p. 142, on this point.

24. ***Life and Diary,*** pp. 244–45.

25. See Chapters Two and Eight on this point. See also ***Be Ye Transformed,*** p. 105.

26. ***Life and Diary,*** p. 219.

27. ***Life and Diary,*** p. 229.

28. ***Life and Diary,*** p. 229.

29. ***Life and Diary,*** pp. 262–63.

30. ***Life and Diary,*** p. 263.

31. ***Life and Diary,*** p. 264.

Chapter Five

1. Gary A. Kellner, "The Innovative Awakener: George Whitefield and the Growth of the Evangelical Revival," available on the web at www.ag.org/enrichmentjournal/199704/078_whitefield.cfm.

2. Frank Lambert, ***"Pedlar in Divinity": George Whitefield and the Transatlantic Revivals*** (Princeton, N.J.: Princeton University Press, 1994), pp. 95–96.

3. ***George Whitefield's Journals*** (Guilford and London: Banner of Truth Trust, 1960), p. 487. Originally published in seven separate volumes 1738–41.

4. Dorothy Loa McFadden, *The Presbyterian Church, Basking Ridge, New Jersey: A History,* 1961, p. 11.

5. Washington Irving, *George Washington: A Biography* (New York: Da Capo Press, 1994), p. 321. Originally published in 1856 as *The Life of George Washington.*

6. *History of Somerset County, New Jersey* (Somerville, N.J.: 1885), p. 744.

7. *The Presbyterian Church, Basking Ridge, New Jersey: A History,* pp. 14–15.

8. Quoted in Arnold A. Dallimore, *George Whitefield: God's Anointed Servant in the Great Revival of the Eighteenth Century* (Wheaton, Ill.: Crossway Books, 1990), p. 18.

9. "The Innovative Awakener," p. 1.

10. *"Pedlar in Divinity,"* p. 96.

11. Mark Noll, *The Rise of Evangelicalism: The Age of Edwards, Whitefield, and the Wesleys* (Downers Grove, Ill.: InterVarsity Press, 2003), pp. 107–8.

12. Howard F. Vos, *Introduction to Church History* (Nashville, Tenn.: Thomas Nelson Publishers, 1994), p. 229.

13. This is a statement made by E. Brooks Holifield in his book, *Theology in America: Christian Thought from the Age of the Puritans to the Civil War* (New Haven, Conn.: Yale University Press, 2003), p. 99.

14. *Memoirs of Jonathan Edwards,* Chapter XII, p. cxiii.

15. *The Rise of Evangelicalism,* pp. 105–6.

16. Quoted in Dallimore, *George Whitefield: God's Anointed Servant,* p. 120.

17. *George Whitefield's Journals,* pp. 343–44.

18. In Kennington, England, for example, he wrote the following journal entry for May 6, 1739: "Went to public worship morning and evening; and, at six, preached at Kennington. Such a sight I never saw before. I believe there were no less than fifty thousand people, and near fourscore coaches, besides great numbers of

horses. There was an awful silence amongst them. God gave me great enlargement of heart. I continued my discourse for an hour and a half, and when I returned home, I was filled with such love, peace, and joy, that I cannot express it. I believe this was partly owing to some opposition I met with yesterday." *George White-field's Journals,* p. 262.
19. *George Whitefield's Journals,* pp. 293–94.
20. Stephen Mansfield, *Forgotten Founding Father: The Heroic Legacy of George Whitefield* (Nashville, Tenn.: Highland Books, 2001), p. 31.

Chapter Six

1. W. Woodford Clayton, *History of Union and Middlesex Counties, New Jersey* (Philadelphia: Everts & Peck, 1882), p. 345.
2. There are amazing similarities between the collapse of the balcony at the Presbyterian church at New Providence and a parallel event that happened at Jonathan Edwards' church in Northampton in 1737. In both situations the balcony collapsed during the Sunday morning service, and no serious injuries occurred in either congregation. It is also interesting to note that the Northampton balcony collapse occurred at the same time that the New Providence sanctuary was being constructed. Edwards' account of the Northampton balcony collapse is noteworthy:

Northampton, March 19, 1737
We in this town, were the last Lord's Day the spectators, and many of us the subjects, of one of the most amazing instances of divine preservation, that perhaps was ever known in the land. Our meeting-house is old and decayed, so that we have been for some time building a new one, which is yet unfinished. . . . [I]n the midst of the public exercise in the forenoon, soon after the beginning of sermon, the whole gallery—full of people, with all the seats and

timber, suddenly and without any warning—sunk, and fell down with the most amazing noise upon the heads of those that sat under, to the astonishment of the congregation. The house was filled with dolorous shrieking and crying; and nothing else was expected than to find many people dead, and dashed to pieces. . . .

But so mysteriously and wonderfully did it come to pass, that every life was preserved; and though many were greatly bruised, and their flesh torn, yet there is not, as I can understand, one bone broken or so much as put out of joint, among them all. Some who were thought to be almost dead at first, were greatly recovered; and but one young woman seems yet to remain in dangerous circumstances, by an inward hurt in her breast: but of late there appears more hope of her recovery.

None can give account, or conceive, by what means people's lives and limbs should be thus preserved, when so great a multitude were thus imminently exposed. It looked as though it was impossible but that great numbers must instantly be crushed to death, or dashed in pieces. It seems unreasonable to ascribe it to any thing else but the care of Providence, in disposing the motions of every piece of timber, and the precise place of safety where every one should sit, and fall, when none were in any capacity to care for their own preservation. The preservation seems to be most wonderful, with respect to the women and children in the middle ally, under the gallery, where it came down first, and with greatest force, and where there was nothing to break the force of the falling weight.

Such an event may be a sufficient argument of a divine Providence over the lives of men.

—Jonathan Edwards, "A Faithful Narrative of the Surprising Work of God," in **The Works of Jonathan Edwards,** Part I, pp. 345–46.

3. *History of Union and Middlesex Counties,* p. 356. The town was renamed from "Turkey" to "New Providence" about 1809 (see page 345 for details).

4. *History of Union and Middlesex Counties,* p. 357.

5. Ezra Squier Tipple, *Francis Asbury: The Prophet of the Long Road* (New York: The Methodist Book Concern, 1916).

6. "Francis Asbury: America's Foremost Circuit Rider," Glimpses #141, Christian History Institute, Warminster, Penn. Available at www.gospelcom.net website.

7. This account was written by his descendant, Stephen S. Day, at the centennial of Methodism in New Providence on September 29, 1898. The paper "Methodism in New Providence" is available at the Rutgers University Library historical archives. For a biography of Stephen Day, see the website www.columbiagypsy.net/steday.htm.

8. Francis Asbury, *The Journal and Letters of Francis Asbury,* Elmer T. Clark, editor-in-chief (Nashville, Tenn.: Abingdon Press, 1958), entry of July 4, 1806, emphasis original.

9. For an informative overview of camp meetings, see the video, "Methodist Camp Meetings," by Vision Video, www.visionvideo.com.

10. *The Journal and Letters of Francis Asbury,* July 5, 1806.

11. *History of Union and Middlesex Counties,* p. 358.

12. *History of Union and Middlesex Counties,* p. 358.

13. "Methodism in New Providence," p. 6.

14. "Methodism in New Providence," p. 14.

15. See Bennet Tyler, *New England Revivals as They Existed at the Close of the Eighteenth and the Beginning of the Nineteenth Centuries* (Wheaton, Ill.: Richard Owen Roberts Publishers, 1980).

16. *Prophet of the Long Road,* pp. 192–94.

17. *Prophet of the Long Road,* pp. 201–4.

18. *Prophet of the Long Road,* pp. 219–20.

19. *Prophet of the Long Road,* p. 313.

20. *Prophet of the Long Road,* pp. 180–82.

21. *Prophet of the Long Road,* pp. 266–67.
22. *Prophet of the Long Road,* pp. 325–26.
23. *Prophet of the Long Road,* pp. 314–16.
24. *Prophet of the Long Road,* p. 309.

Chapter Seven

1. Rev. Talbot W. Chambers, *The New York City Noon Prayer Meeting* (Colorado Springs, Col.: Wagner Publications, 2002), p. 111.
2. Quoted by Rev. Oliver W. Price in "The Layman's Prayer Revival of 1857–1858," which is published at the website bpf.gospelcom.net/layman.html.
3. *The New York City Noon Prayer Meeting,* p. 29.
4. Samuel I. Prime, *The Power of Prayer* (Carlisle, Penn.: Banner of Truth, 1998), pp. 4–5. Originally published in 1859.
5. *The Power of Prayer,* pp. 7–8.
6. *The Power of Prayer,* p. 8.
7. *The Power of Prayer,* p. 10.
8. *The New York City Noon Prayer Meeting,* p. 38.
9. *The Power of Prayer,* pp. 16–17.
10. *The Power of Prayer,* pp. 25–26.
11. Bill Tucker and Tim Crosby, "The Day of Small Things," DoorWays Radiobroadcast Sermon, The Quiet Hour, Redlands, Calif., 2001. Available at www.thequiethour.org.
12. "The Layman's Prayer Revival of 1857–1858."
13. Elmer Towns and Douglas Porter, *The Ten Greatest Revivals Ever* (Ann Arbor, Mich.: Servant Publications, 2000), pp. 122–26.
14. Charles Haddon Spurgeon, *Revival Year Sermons* (Carlisle, Penn.: The Banner of Truth, 2002). Originally published by Banner of Truth Trust in 1959.
15. Martyn Lloyd-Jones, *Revival* (Wheaton, Ill.: Crossway Books, 1987), pp. 7–8.
16. *The Power of Prayer,* pp. 13–14.

Chapter Eight

1. J. A. Motyer, *The Message of Isaiah* (Downers Grove, Ill.: InterVarsity Press, 1996), pp. 145–46, emphasis original.
2. Ed Silvoso, *Prayer Evangelism* (Ventura, Calif.: Gospel Light Publications, 2000) and *Anointed for Business* (Ventura, Calif.: Gospel Light Publications, 2002); Rich Marshall, *God @ Work* (Shippensberg, Penn.: Destiny Image, 1999); Rick Heeren, *Thank God It's Monday!* (San Jose, Calif.: Transformational Publications, 2004); Jack Serra, *Marketplace, Marriage, and Revival: The Spiritual Connection* (Orlando, Fla.: Longwood Communications, 2001).
3. Chuck Pierce message to the New Jersey Strategic Prayer Network on August 21, 2002. A transcription of this message is available at the website for the Church of Grace and Peace, Toms River, N.J.: www.graceandpeace.org.
4. Dr. Suuqiina, *Can You Feel the Mountains Tremble? A Healing the Land Handbook* (Anchorage, Alaska: Inuit Ministries International, 1999), pp. 92–93.
5. Taken from Ed Silvoso, *Anointed for Business,* pp. 87–88, with original scripture references from the NASB.
6. Jonathan Edwards, *Thoughts on the Revival,* Part V, Sect. III, p. 428.
7. See also Note 2 above re *Prayer Evangelism.*
8. William C. Conant, *Narratives of Remarkable Conversions and Revival Incidents: Including a Review of Revivals from the Day of Pentecost to the Great Awakening of the last century—Conversions of eminent persons—Instances of remarkable conversions and answers to prayers—An account of the rise and progress of the Great Awakening of 1857–'8* (New York: Derby & Jackson, 1858), pp. 357–60.
9. *Narratives of Remarkable Conversions and Revival Incidents,* pp. 368–69.

Chapter Nine

1. *Memoirs of Jonathan Edwards,* Chapter XII, pp. cxv–cxvi.

2. This analysis is based on the article "Praying in the Four Winds of God for Revivals," by Pastor Peter Tan from Eagle Vision Ministries. The weblink for this article is www.eaglevision.com.my/ps28four.htm. His observations are based on an earlier book by Norvel Hayes, *The Winds of God Bring Revival* (Tulsa, Okla.: Harrison House, 1985).

3. *Memoirs of Jonathan Edwards,* Chapter XIII, p. cxxi, letter dated March 5, 1744.

Chapter Ten

1. "Full Text of Robert Juet's Journal," from the collections of the New York Historical Society, Second Series, 1841. Available at www.newsday.com/community/guide/lihistory/ny-history-hs216a1v,0,919043.story.

2. Edwin G. Burrows and Mike Wallace, *Gotham* (New York: Oxford University Press, 1999), pp. 3–4.

3. From the website www.studio2b.org/escape/greenscene/time_traveling.asp.

4. See Burrows and Wallace, *Gotham,* pp. xiv–xvi for a discussion of this transaction.

5. *Gotham,* p. 38.

6. *Gotham,* pp. 37–40.

7. *A History of the City of Newark: Embracing Practically Two and a Half Centuries, 1666–1913,* Volume I (New York and Chicago: The Lewis Historical Publishing Company, 1913), p. 57 (no author).

8. *A History of the City of Newark,* p. 189.

9. See David Bryant, *Christ Is All!: A Joyous Manifesto on the Supremacy of God's Son* (New Providence, N.J.: New Providence Publishers, Second Edition, 2005).

10. Ed Silvoso discusses this point in *Anointed for Business* (Ventura, Calif.: Regal Books, 2002), p. 74.

11. But note that God reverses the order in 2 Chronicles 7:14, when He promises to heal the people before healing the land. The author would like to thank Dave Thompson for this insight.

12. Alistair Petrie, *Releasing Heaven on Earth: Principles for Healing the Land* (Grand Rapids, Mich.: Chosen Books, 2000), pp. 57–64.

13. Alistair Petrie, *A Sacred Trust: An interactive workbook for those seeking an in-depth study of the issues of the theology and stewardship of the land, revival, and transformation* (Kelowna, B.C.: Partnership Ministries, 2004), p. 49.

14. *A Sacred Trust,* p. 56.

15. See reports from the Global Day of Prayer website at www.globaldayofprayer.com and www.transformationafrica.org.

16. *National Geographic,* September 2005, "Africa: Whatever you thought, think again." The lead article in this issue states, "This is the place where, two and a half million years ago, humans and animals first converged, sharing some of earth's most spectacular ground. Today, with competition for resources on the rise, convergence has become collision, fueling war, disease, and extinction. Yet despite such calamities, Africa is alive with stories of renewal" (p. 3).

17. From Graham Power's lecture on "Transformation Africa" presented at the 14th International Institute on Prayer Evangelism, Mar del Plata, Argentina, November 2004.

18. See *Christian History* Issue 45 (1995), "Camp Meetings & Circuit Riders." Back issues of this publication are available from Christianity Today, 465 Gunderson Drive, Carol Stream IL 60188.

Scripture Index

General Index

Redigging America's wells of revival

HIGHWAYS
of
HOLINESS
Prayer Guide

40 readings compiled
by Lloyd Turner

For more information about how to declare you own Highway of Holiness, or to purchase a copy of the **Highways of Holiness Prayer Guide**, please contact the author at:

Lloyd Turner, Ph.D.
The Caring Network
PO Box 872
New Providence, NJ 07974 USA

Or by email at:
HighwaysOfHoliness@verizon.net